CULTURE SMART!
SOUTH AFRICA

David Holt-Biddle

·K·U·P·E·R·A·R·D·

First published in Great Britain 2007
by Kuperard, an imprint of Bravo Ltd
59 Hutton Grove, London N12 8DS
Tel: +44 (0) 20 8446 2440 Fax: +44 (0) 20 8446 2441
www.culturesmartguides.com
Inquiries: sales@kuperard.co.uk

Culture Smart! is a registered trademark of Bravo Ltd

Distributed in the United States and Canada
by Random House Distribution Services
1745 Broadway, New York, NY 10019
Tel: +1 (212) 572-2844 Fax: +1 (212) 572-4961
Inquiries: csorders@randomhouse.com

Series Editor Geoffrey Chesler
Design Bobby Birchall

ISBN 978 1 85733 346 6

British Library Cataloguing in Publication Data
A CIP catalogue entry for this book is available from the
British Library

Printed in Malaysia

Cover image: Greenmarket Square, Cape Town. *South African Tourist Board*
The painting on page 123, *Saxophonist*, by Oliver Caldecott, is reproduced by kind
permission of Moyra Caldecott.
Images reproduced by permission of South African Tourist Board on the following
pages: 12, 35, 41, 42, 54, 55, 59, 69, 94, 101, 106, 112, 115, 116, 121, 125, 128, 141.

CultureSmart!Consulting and Culture Smart! guides have both
contributed to and featured regularly in the weekly travel program
"Fast Track" on BBC World TV.

About the Author

DAVID HOLT-BIDDLE is an award-winning freelance journalist who has lived in South Africa for most of his life. He has traveled much of the world, including Africa, both on assignment and independently. He has worked in radio, television, and the print media as a reporter, editor, producer, and presenter, and has coauthored two books. His main interests are the environment, travel, history, and archaeology.

Other Books in the Series

Other titles are in preparation. For more information, contact: info@kuperard.co.uk

The publishers would like to thank **CultureSmart!**Consulting for its help in researching and developing the concept for this series.

CultureSmart!Consulting creates tailor-made seminars and consultancy programs to meet a wide range of corporate, public-sector, and individual needs. Whether delivering courses on multicultural team building in the U.S.A., preparing Chinese engineers for a posting in Europe, training call-center staff in India, or raising the awareness of police forces to the needs of diverse ethnic communities, we provide essential, practical, and powerful skills worldwide to an increasingly international workforce.

For details, visit www.culturesmartconsulting.com

contents

contents

Map of South Africa

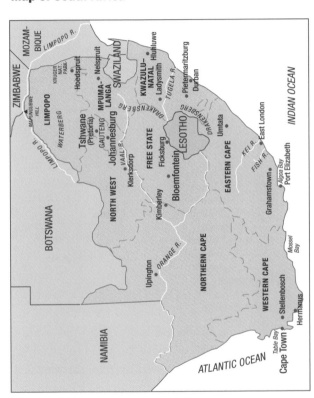

introduction

Generalizations about South Africa would be dangerous. In such a country, with eleven official languages, nine major Black African tribes, two major White tribes, and a host of other peoples, as well as a representation of all the world's major religions, who would dare generalize? In such a country, where there is major gender inequality, yet where the Deputy President and a third of the Cabinet are women, where Communists sit in Parliament yet a free market economy rules, where there are very, very rich, and very, very poor, of all races, who would dare generalize? In fact, forget just about everything you have ever heard about South Africa. There are a lot of surprises here.

South Africa has been described as a "World in One Country" and a "Rainbow Nation"; but is the curate's egg all good, all bad, or good and bad in parts? For years the rest of the world willed South Africa to implode, yet after a remarkably troubled time, when it looked as though civil war were the only route left, a new South Africa emerged, a South Africa with one of the most liberal and comprehensive constitutions in the world, a South Africa with a will to survive as a united nation, a South Africa with hope.

There are major problems, such as crime and HIV/AIDS, and in some instances the apparent loss of old values, in favor of the new. As Sue Derwent puts it in her book *Peoples of the South*, "With the onslaught of modernism and Western culture, many traditions are being eroded by the demands of an increasingly industrialised and cosmopolitan society. Many beautiful and ancient customs and practices, once integral to traditional African culture, survive only as tourist attractions. Unless all the peoples of southern Africa honour the spirits of their ancestors and nurture their age-old conventions and wisdom, in time, they could be lost forever."

So South Africa stands on the cusp of the old and the new, the First and the Third Worlds, the North and the South. This book will introduce you to a vibrant society in transition. It examines the often painful past to explain some of the complexities and contradictions of modern South African society. It looks at how people relate to each other, at home, work, and play, and offers advice on what to expect and how to behave in different contexts. South Africans are big-hearted and optimistic. Make the effort to understand them and they will welcome you unreservedly.

Key Facts

Official Name	The Republic of South Africa	
Capital Cities	Tshwane (formerly Pretoria), the administrative capital; Cape Town, the legislative capital, and Bloemfontein, the judicial capital	
Major Cities	Johannesburg, including Soweto (pop. 3.2 million); eThekweni (the Durban complex – pop. 2.5 m); Cape Town (pop. 2.9 m); Tshwane (pop. 2 m); Nelson Mandela (the Port Elizabeth complex – pop. 1 m)	
Area	470, 693 sq. miles (1,219,090 sq. km)	
Climate	Semidesert to subtropical, but largely moderate	The southwestern Cape has a Mediterranean-type climate.
Land Use	About 15 percent is considered arable, although vast stretches are suitable for stock ranching.	The southwestern Cape is heavily cultivated.
Currency	Rand = 100 cents	
Population	Approximately 45 million (2001 census)	
Ethnic Makeup	Black 79%, White 9.6%, Colored (mixed race) 8.9%, Asian 2.5% (2001)	
Age Structure	10–14, 5.06 m; 15–19, 4.99 m; 5–9, 4.85 m; 50–65, 3.9 m	
Language	11 official languages. English most widely spoken	

Main Religions	Mainly Christian (about 80%) and African traditional, and small percentages of Islam, Hinduism, Judaism	
Government	Constitutional democracy with a three-tier system: executive, legislative, and independent judiciary	
Media	State-owned television and radio channels, two independent TV channels, and many radio channels, and a very free newspaper scene (20 dailies, 13 weeklies)	English is the main language of communication for TV and radio, and daily and weekly newspapers in all main centers.
Electricity	220 volts, 50 Hz	Mainly coal-burning power stations and one nuclear station
TV/Video	PAL system	
Telephone	Country code 27	Dial out 09. Three-digit area code must always be dialed when phoning locally. Three mobile phone networks
Time	GMT +2 hours	

LAND & PEOPLE

A WORLD IN ONE COUNTRY

"A World in One Country" was a term coined by the South African tourism authorities some time ago, and it is remarkably apt. Geographically, South Africa occupies the southern tip of the continent of Africa. Its jagged northern border is shared by Namibia, Botswana, Zimbabwe, Swaziland, and Mozambique, and it completely surrounds Lesotho. On the western side is the Atlantic Ocean

and on the eastern and southern sides the Indian Ocean. Its main feature is a high central plateau that covers much of the country and sweeps up toward the north, surrounded by a mountain bulwark dividing it from the mostly narrow coastal plain to the east, the south, and the southwest, with a gradual falling off from the high plateau toward the west. There are few major rivers and even the biggest, the Orange, may be reduced to a trickle by frequent drought. Many rivers are seasonal, and there are no major freshwater lakes.

In terms of geographic diversity, however, it is indeed a World in One Country. There are great mountains, snow-covered in winter, vast plains of grassland, or scrub (the famous *veld*), with its roving wildlife, miles and miles of bush, and tracts of desert with red sand dunes. The fertile coastal plain ranges from some of the southernmost coral reefs in the world in a subtropical setting in the east, to stretches of indigenous forests in the south, the Mediterranean-like region and the wine lands in the southwest, and the arid but starkly beautiful West Coast. And there are beaches everywhere.

CLIMATE

South Africa's location in the Southern Hemisphere obviously makes its seasons the reverse of those in the Northern Hemisphere, so the height of the South African summer is December/January, and midwinter is June/July. The climate is generally moderate. The country is geographically described as a semiarid zone with an average annual rainfall of less than 20 inches (around 500 mm)—the world average is about

33 inches (around 850 mm). About two-thirds of the country have less than the average, but the extremes in the highs and lows range from as much as 79 inches (2,000 mm) to as little as 2 inches (50 mm). The central plateau has hot, wettish summers and cold, dry winters, while the coastal belt tends to be more temperate. The southwestern Cape has a decidedly Mediterranean climate with winter rainfall, allowing for grape, olive, and deciduous fruit industries (which is not to say that grapes are not grown elsewhere in South Africa). Snow falls on the high mountains in winter.

TEMPERATURES

Temperatures seldom exceed 95°F (35°C) in the warm zones or 23°F (-5°C) in the coldest, although there are clearly exceptions. Approximate average maximums and minimums are:

Johannesburg, Gauteng, South Africa's commercial hub:
77°/36.7°F (25°/2.6°C)

Kimberley, capital of the Northern Cape:
89.6°/34.7°F (32°/1.5°C)

Cape Town, capital of the Western Cape:
79.7°/44.6°F (26.5°/7°C)

Pietermaritzburg, capital of KwaZulu–Natal, about 80 km from Durban: **82.4°/43.3°F (28°/6.3°C)**

A BRIEF HISTORY

South Africa's human history began about 2.3 million years ago with *Homo habilis*, the first in the human genus, *Homo*. He lived in the Sterkfontein Valley, which is now a World Heritage Site, known as the Cradle of Humankind, near Johannesburg. This fellow continued to evolve through many stages, including *Homo erectus*, who, brandishing his stone tools, was the first to march out of Africa to populate the world, between about 400,000 and two million years ago. Evolution continued to play its part and between 100,000 and 200,000 years ago *Homo sapiens*, anatomically modern man, evolved. Those who stayed in southern Africa are the direct ancestors of the San, or Bushmen, who may still be found in South Africa today. They were hunter-gatherers, and in some parts of southern Africa they still are.

Next on the scene in southern Africa, about two thousand years ago, were the KhoiKhoi, pastoralists who (according to two different schools of thought) either migrated down from the north or culturally evolved from the San. They are certainly of similar physical appearance. The San and the KhoiKhoi were in southern Africa when the first Iron Age Bantu speakers (Black Africans) began arriving in the first 250 years of the Common Era.

We must now make another leap forward, across nearly 1,500 years. The San, the KhoiKhoi, and the Black Africans were uncomfortably sharing what was to become South Africa, with the San just about everywhere, the Blacks mainly in the north, center, east, and southeast, and the KhoiKhoi mainly in the west, the south, and the southeast. That was the situation when Europeans first set foot on the African subcontinent.

A Legacy of Conflict

The history of South Africa has been marked by conflict. Two thousand years ago the KhoiKhoi upset the tranquility of the hunter-gatherer life for the San, and not more than a couple of hundred years later the arrival of the first of the Black Iron Age peoples from the north had everyone at odds. Although there was a degree of coexistence, this conflict over land and resources (both the KhoiKhoi and the Blacks had cattle and needed land for them, and the San believed the land belonged to no one) lasted until well after the arrival of the White man. Sadly, virtually the first contact between Whites and locals in South Africa was one of violence. The Portuguese mariner-explorers were looking for fresh water, the KhoiKhoi believed they owned the water source, and there was a brief and bloody fight. With the arrival of the Dutch at the Cape in the seventeenth century there was soon conflict with all those already there. This clash of cultures led to a series of ongoing frontier wars between the parties, conflicts that continued after the British takeover in the early nineteenth century.

Slavery was always a fact (it had existed in Africa from time immemorial, from long before the White man's appearance), but it became more of an immediate issue in South Africa when the British abolished it throughout the Empire in 1834, and many of the more recalcitrant Dutch settlers decided to leave the Cape Colony rather than submit to British suzerainty (though many elected to stay). These were the *Voortrekkers*

(those "who go before"). They of course clashed with the many different Black African tribes occupying the interior, and their advance was marked by great battles and minor wars.

Of course, the Black tribes were also in conflict with each other because of the ravages of the *mfecane* ("crushing" or "grinding"). This was the

THE JERUSALEM GANGERS

One of the groups of *trekkers* was known as the Jerusalem *Gangers* (travelers). They were convinced that the British in the Cape were representatives of the Antichrist and were determined to get as far away from them as possible. They set their sights on Israel. Some of their old family Bibles contained maps that showed Africa, Egypt, and Israel, so they began on the right track. Up in the north of South Africa they came upon a lively stream; they thought they had reached North Africa, and named their stream *De Nyl*, the Nile. In fact so confident were they that they even declared this to be the source of this mighty river, and named it *De Nyl Zyn Oog* (the Eye of the Nile)! Their imaginations were fed by other physical features of the area, however, including the massive and brooding Kranskop Mountain, which the Jerusalem *Gangers*, tired, far from home, and longing for Israel, thought might be the remnants of one of the great pyramids of Egypt. Sadly, they still had nearly four thousand miles to go.

violent domino effect that had been set in motion by that Napoleon of Africa, Shaka of the Zulus. The *mfecane* swept eastern, central, and northern southern Africa, depopulating vast tracts of land and reaching as far as Tanzania in the north and as far as Botswana in the west. There were to be constant hostilities over land between the ever-mobile Dutch

Boers (literally, "farmers"), the colonizing British, and the settled, and often roving, Black tribes. There were two wars between the Boer republics and the British, leaving a hatred that survived well into the second

half of the twentieth century. In all of this everyone persecuted the San. They were generally considered "different," and they were also inveterate cattle thieves, believing that cattle, like land, belonged to no one. Such was the course of a turbulent history.

Slavery eventually became a thing of the past, and colonialism in its true form died with the creation of the Union of South Africa in 1910, but their legacies lived on. The legacy that became Apartheid (the hated state system of racial separation) was disappearing by the 1980s, and its final death knell was the elections of April 1994. Although faded, or blunted, however, memories of many centuries of conflict linger.

A CHRONOLOGY OF KEY EVENTS

1488 The Portuguese explorer Bartolomeu Dias landed at Mossel Bay, but did not stay.

1652 Hollander Jan van Riebeeck arrived in Table Bay to establish a revictualing station for the Dutch East India Company (the VOC). Soon after, the first slaves, from Dutch settlements in the Far East and from the east coast of Africa, were brought in to provide labor.

1690 Dutch farmers and "free burghers" (former VOC employees who had gained their independence and turned to farming) began spreading outward from the revictualing station and clashed with the KhoiKhoi pastoralists.

1690–1770s Dutch expansion gradually turned the revictualing station into a colony, and by the 1770s there were clashes with the most southerly of the Black groups, the Xhosa, around the Fish River in what is now the Eastern Cape, the eastern extent of the Dutch settlers and the southern extent of the Xhosa.

1795 In a flurry of colonial exchanges brought about by the Napoleonic Wars in Europe, Britain annexed the Dutch Cape Colony; in 1803 the Dutch took it back; and in 1805 the British reclaimed it.

1816 Shaka became king of the newly formed Zulu nation and the *mfecane*, or *difacane*, began. The warlike Zulus began to expand and drive other peoples before them, an effect felt throughout much of southern Africa.

1820 The first group of British settlers arrived in Algoa Bay in the Eastern Cape.

1834 Britain abolished slavery throughout the Empire, including South Africa, and one of the most significant events in South Africa's history, the Great Trek of Dutch out of the Cape into the interior of southern Africa, began.

1838–54 Various Boer (Dutch) republics, including the Transvaal and the Orange Free State, were established in the interior, and the British colony of Natal was established on the east coast. These were years of conflict between Boer, Briton, and Black.

1860 The first indentured laborers arrived from India to work on the sugarcane plantations of Natal.

1867 Diamonds were discovered in the northern Cape.

1879 The Anglo-Zulu War, ending with the British subjugation of the Zulus.

1880–81 The first Anglo-Boer War, ending with independence for the Transvaal Republic.

1886 Gold was discovered on the Witwatersrand; Johannesburg was founded.

1899–1902 The South African War (second Anglo-Boer War), the culmination of years of tensions between Boers and British, dragging in most of the country and most of its peoples.

1910 The South African Union was established, uniting the former republics of the Transvaal and the Orange Free State, and the former British colonies of the Cape and Natal, into one country as a dominion within the British Empire.

From Union to Apartheid

The period from 1910 to 1948 was a momentous one, seeing the development of the Old South Africa and the entry of most of the players in the run-up to what would eventually become the New South Africa. The Union was basically a "White" state, with "Black" affairs left to the provincial governments (the two former republics and the two former colonies), a move seen as a fundamental betrayal of Black African aspirations.

1912 The African National Congress (ANC) was established to represent Black African interests.

1913 The Native Land Act limited Black land ownership.

1914 South Africa joined the Allies in the Great War, and the National Party (NP), representing Afrikaner (as the Boers were now known), anti-British interests, was established.

1920 The South African Indian Congress, representing Indian interests, was founded.

1921 The Communist Party of South Africa and the Afrikaner Broederbond, a secret brotherhood, were formed.

1930s Much legislation separating the races was introduced. Some of the harshest measures came in 1936, when Blacks were removed from the common voters' roll in the Cape and the Native Trust and Land Act limited Blacks to ownership of just 13 percent of the land.

1939–45 With much opposition from many Afrikaners, South Africa joined the Allies in the Second World War, but South Africans of all communities flocked to volunteer to go "Up North" to fight. At home in 1944 the ANC Youth League was formed.

1946 General Jan Smuts's United Party introduced legislation to curtail the activities of Indians. The newly formed United Nations (Smuts was a founding father) took note of the South African situation for the first time.

1948 The National Party defeated the United Party in a general election and the Apartheid era began.

From Apartheid to Insurrection

The time from 1948 to 1976 saw a changing face of South Africa, a period in which the policy of Apartheid, or "separate racial development" was entrenched in the early years. *Apartheid* means "separateness" in Afrikaans, and the basic concept was to have the various races developing separately, but equally, in their own territories. Of course some, namely the Whites, were to be "more equal than others." Possibly the most draconian measure was the Population Registration Act (1950), which decided who belonged to which race. The foundation was laid now for building the walls.

1952 The ANC launched its defiance campaign as legislation became more and more repressive.

1955 The Freedom Charter was adopted by the Congress of the People.

1959 The Pan Africanist Congress (PAC) was established. (The PAC was formed as a breakaway from the ANC. Influenced by the Africanist ideals of Ghana's Kwame Nkrumah, it promotes the return of the land to the indigenous people.)

1960 The Sharpeville massacre; 69 people were killed in a PAC and ANC organized anti-pass laws demonstration.

1961 Prime Minister Verwoerd, after a narrowly won referendum the year before, created a republic, and South Africa's membership of the Commonwealth was immediately terminated. In that same year the ANC's armed wing, Umkhonto weSizwe, was established.

1964 The Rivonia Treason Trial ended and Nelson Mandela and many other ANC leaders were sent to Robben Island.

1966 Prime Minister Verwoerd was assassinated by a deranged Mozambiquan-Greek parliamentary messenger, Demetrios Tsafendas, and B. J. Vorster took over.

1975 Inkatha, a Zulu cultural/political movement, was set up by Mangosutho Buthelezi, and South Africa became involved in the Angolan War.

1976 The Transkei, the first of the so-called Bantustans (Black tribal homelands provided by Apartheid legislation), gained its independence. The Soweto

Uprising began. This was a revolt by Black school pupils against the use of Afrikaans as a medium of instruction in their schools. This ushered in the end of an era.

From Soweto to Democracy

1976–90 These were tumultuous years. The UN instituted an arms embargo; political organizations and newspapers were banned; Vorster resigned; P. W. Botha took over; a White referendum approved limited reforms, including a separate franchise for Coloreds and Indians; COSATU (Congress of South African Trade Unions) was established in 1985. In 1989 Botha and Mandela met; Botha resigned; and F. W. de Klerk took over. In 1990 De Klerk lifted the ban on the ANC, the PAC, the SACP, and thirty other opposition groups; and released Mandela from prison.

1990–94 The situation developed rapidly. The ANC suspended the armed struggle. In 1991 the NP government and the ANC agreed on all-party negotiations; important Apartheid legislation was repealed. In 1992 a White referendum gave De Klerk the go-ahead to negotiate for a New South Africa, a Record of Understanding was signed, introducing the concept of an elected interim government of national unity. In 1993, Communist Party Secretary General Chris Hani was assassinated by right-wingers and the country came to the brink of civil war, but just in time a transitional constitution was accepted, providing for a nonracial, multiparty democracy and elections were called for 1994.

April 27, 1994 The African National Congress, in an alliance with the South African Communist Party and the Congress of South African Trade Unions, won South Africa's first fully democratic elections.

TRANSITION AND THE RACE CARD

Few countries in the world have experienced what South Africa has gone through over the past two decades. The beginning of the end of the old regime probably came on June 16, 1976, when the children of Soweto marched against Afrikaans as the language used in schools. This led to open and often bloody conflict through the rest of the 1970s and the '80s. Many people fled the country to settle in greener pastures, and many went into exile. By the end of the '80s there was a sense of hopelessness, a feeling that things could only get worse. Then in February 1990 President F. W. de Klerk surprised just about everyone, lifting the ban on the ANC and releasing Mandela, and suddenly the goalposts had been moved.

It's all history now, but what history does not describe is the atmosphere, the feeling at the time. There were endless negotiations, endless threats, and a little action, from the Far Right Wing, and there was endless fear of what the new dispensation might bring—retribution from the Blacks, a massive backlash from the Whites? The country was walking a tightrope, and then in April 1993 the Communist leader Chris Hani was assassinated. The tightrope was given a vigorous shaking and the country came closer to a holocaust than it had ever come before. Somehow, and perhaps no one really knows just how, the tightrope steadied and the country moved back from the brink and toward the elections of April 1994. To quote a leading journalist, Denis Beckett, at the time, "March 1994 was an exciting month, all right, with a new nation about to be born. But there were jitters too, big-league jitters. Would the army mutiny? Would the right-wing stage a putsch? Would Inkatha unleash impis [regiments of Zulu warriors]? And—shudder—what if just one random assassin got to either of the figures on center stage, F. W. de Klerk or Nelson?" It was indeed jittery.

And then came Election Day. The country held its breath. Millions began lining up before dawn,  virtually all of them about to cast their first-ever ballot in a democratic election. No one who voted that day will ever forget it, and everyone has his or her own story. Amazingly, the day passed without serious incident, but the country continued to hold its breath while the election dragged on for several more days. Eventually, however, the result was announced. The ANC had triumphed, and the New South Africa had arrived.

THE RAINBOW NATION

"The Rainbow Nation" was a term first used by Nobel Peace Prize Winner Archbishop Desmond Tutu, around the time of the birth of the new South Africa, and therefore a new nation. The term is a celebration of the distinctive racial and cultural mix that is South Africa.

Under the old system South Africans were divided into four groups: Blacks, Whites, Coloreds, and Asians. Paradoxically, many official documents still have a box for "race." Anyway, although they are today one nation, this is more or less the way South Africans see themselves— but we need to make a large number of sub-pigeonholes.

Although there are around 46.9 million South Africans, it is safe to say that there is no such thing as a typical South African. There are, for example, eleven official languages, but many more are spoken, and there is a great diversity of racial types, tribes, cultures, religions, and ways of doing things. The status of the population is currently thus: Blacks, 37.2 million, or 79.4 percent; Whites 4.4 million, or 9.3 percent; Coloreds 4.1 million, or 8.8 percent; Asians 1.1 million, or 2.5 percent.

Black South Africans

Black South Africans, those people of purely African descent, may be roughly divided into two main groups, the Nguni and the Sotho. Both groups descend from Bantu language speakers who emigrated down the continent from west-central Africa, with the Nguni staying in the east and southeast and the Sotho doubling back from the main southward movement to settle mainly in the central and northern parts of the country. The Nguni are the Zulu, the Xhosa, the Swazi, and the Ndebele, while the Sotho are the North Sotho, the South Sotho, and the Tswana. There are others, however, like the Shangaan-Tsonga and the Venda, who live in the far northeast of the country, who do not fit neatly into either the Nguni or the Sotho group, but who make up their own grouping. It must be pointed out that these major tribes may be divided into smaller tribes, which in turn may be divided into clans or family groups.

White South Africans
White South Africans may be divided into three main groups: Afrikaners, English-speaking, and others. The Afrikaners are descended from the original Dutch settlers of the seventeenth century, having spread from the Cape across the country. They again may be divided into subcultures, as there are many differences between the Afrikaners of the Southwestern Cape, for example, and the Afrikaners of the interior, the descendants of the *Voortrekkers*.

English-speaking South Africans hail mainly from the second British occupation of the Cape and the influx of the 1820 Settlers and subsequent waves of immigrants. These people, too, spread out across the country as explorers, hunters, missionaries, and farmers. They established the colony of Natal in the nineteenth century, but were also present in the Boer republics in the interior (note the problems with the *Uitlanders* [foreigners] and the discovery of gold in the Transvaal!). Scots, too, came out in large numbers, many of them to carry out missionary work (like Livingstone and Moffat), and are still an important community.

"Others" include the many and vital communities such as the Portuguese, the French, the Germans, and more recently the Italians, the Greeks, and smatterings of other European peoples. The Portuguese, of course, were the first European "discoverers" and explorers of South Africa. Their input was small to begin with, but grew through trade, immigration, and straight assimilation, after the Portuguese colonies in Africa gained their independence following Portugal's peaceful Revolution of 1974. Today the Portuguese community is the largest community of European origin, apart from the Afrikaners and the English, and their contribution to the country is a major one.

French influence in South Africa began with the first wave of Huguenots who were fleeing religious persecution at home in the late seventeenth century. Their influence on Afrikaans culture has been particularly noteworthy, and many Afrikaans surnames are of French origin. Many Germans came out in those early years as well, adding to the European cultural mix. British, French, and Scandinavian explorers and naturalists who came out in the late eighteenth century, in the Age of Enlightenment, made a huge contribution, particularly in the natural sciences. Later, particularly in the twentieth century, the Greek and Italian communities grew to make important contributions to their new society (many Italians came out as prisoners-of-war during the Second World War, and never went home). There are also other important, relatively new communities, including Russians and other East Europeans, many of whom fled the postwar Communist regimes.

The Jewish community has been an important influence over the years. Jews came with van Riebeeck, and more among the 1820 Settlers. The largest number came from Tsarist Russia at the end of the nineteenth century—particularly from Lithuania. They have played an important role in the sciences, especially medicine, and the arts, as well as in the economy, and were among the founders of Johannesburg. They have been, and still are, a vital ingredient in the South African mix.

Colored South Africans

The Colored (still a contentious term) community had its beginnings in liaisons between the early Dutch sojourners and the slaves, and also the Khoisan (see below), and later the Blacks. Today it is a community that stands alone, although it includes, for example, other groups like the Malays, the Namas (originally KhoiKhoi), and the Griquas (originally people with European and KhoiKhoi roots). The KhoiKhoi (later called the Hottentots, no longer a politically correct term) tended to be absorbed into the greater Colored community.

The San

The San, or Bushmen, the original inhabitants of South Africa, could today be described as the Lost People. The lifestyle of the true San, that of the hunter-gatherer, has virtually disappeared, although until less than two decades ago it could still be observed in Botswana and Angola. They may be divided into a dozen different clans or groups, speaking as many languages, and although the government has made efforts to restore some of their "sense of place" in parts of the Kalahari, their future as a distinct culture is at best bleak.

The San and the KhoiKhoi, later collectively referred to as the KhoiSan, are racially distinct from other South Africans, being generally more gracile and lighter in complexion, and often having almost Mongoloid features. The San are, however, unique as representatives of a culture that was once that of all men, the hunter-gatherer. Their languages are also unique, as they have not been traced back to any specific linguistic root.

Asian South Africans
By far the biggest community of Asian origin is the Indian one. The first indentured laborers from India were brought out in 1860 to man the burgeoning sugarcane industry in Natal. They were both Hindu and Muslim—but more of that when we discuss religious diversity. Like the Italians eighty years later, most of them, once their time had been served, elected to stay and make South Africa their home.

The Indian community is by and large very successful, being well represented in just about every sphere of endeavor in South Africa. It is also believed to be one of the largest Indian communities outside India. The most famous of all Indians in this country was Mahatma Gandhi, who was here in the early years of the twentieth century, practicing law, and formulating much of his political thinking around the South African situation. Perhaps following his lead, Indians have been very involved in the South African political scene over the years, and still are. South African Indians speak a wide variety of Indian languages at home, although the *lingua franca,* as it is with most South Africans, is English.

An important, but small, community is the Chinese one. The Chinese have always been a quiet and reserved group, although all major centers have a Chinatown and Chinese restaurants dot the landscape. Like the Indians, the Chinese are well represented in many different spheres, but it is perhaps in medicine that they have excelled.

Illegal Immigrants

And finally, those people who are not South Africans at all—the foreigners. According entirely to the statistics one wants to believe, there could be up to five million illegal aliens in the country. The vast majority of them are from Africa, as the rest of the continent tends to see South Africa as the crock of gold at the end of the rainbow (no pun intended). Many of them are from the SADC (Southern African Development Community) region, particularly Mozambique, Zimbabwe, Lesotho, Swaziland, Malawi, and Zambia, many of whom came to South Africa over the years to work in the gold mines. Vast numbers, however, are from Francophone Africa; in fact, whole areas of Johannesburg are French-speaking. Many others are from Nigeria and elsewhere in West Africa, fewer are from East or North Africa. Illegal or not, they tend to make the street markets and the nightlife more interesting.

A rainbow nation indeed.

GOVERNMENT . . .

The Republic of South Africa is a constitutional democracy. It has a three-tier system of government with the executive, the legislative bodies, and an independent judiciary that is subject only to the constitution and the law, and the constitution is the highest law in the land. The constitution, hammered out in the years after the 1994 election, is considered one of the most progressive in the world, and includes an extensive Bill of Rights. It came into being in 1997.

The executive is headed by the President, currently Thabo Mveliswa Mbeki, the Deputy President, currently Phumzile Mlambo-Ngcuka, and the cabinet, which consists of twenty-five ministers appointed by the President. The President, in turn, is elected from the majority party by the National Assembly. He is the executive Head of State and may not serve for more than two five-year terms.

The legislative authority is parliament, which consists of the National Assembly and the National Council of Provinces (NCP). The National Assembly may have no more than 400 members and they are elected for a five-year term on the basis of a common voters' roll—the voter votes for a party, and the party appoints the Member of Parliament. The National Council of Provinces consists of fifty-four permanent members and thirty-six so-called special delegates, each of the nine provinces (in alphabetical order, Eastern Cape, Free State, Gauteng, KwaZulu–Natal, Limpopo, Mpumalanga, North West, Northern Cape, and Western Cape) sends ten representatives. The NCP participates fully in the legislative process, aligning national and provincial interests and providing the link between provincial legislations and Parliament. Parliament is bound by the constitution.

WHO'S WHO IN THE NATIONAL ASSEMBLY

The standing of the parties in the National Assembly in 2006 was as follows:

The African National Congress: Created to unite Blacks in defense of their rights and to fight for freedom; 279 seats (Members of Parliament), in alliance with the 7 held by the New National Party (the remnants of the original NP, created for much the same reasons as the ANC, except it was for the Afrikaner); giving the ANC a total of 286 seats out of a possible 400, or 70 percent.

Democratic Alliance: Stands for liberal democracy and free market principles; 50 seats.

Inkatha Freedom Party: Largely represents the Zulu in KwaZulu–Natal and elsewhere; 28 seats.

United Democratic Movement: Led by Bantu Holomisa, former military strongman of the Transkei "homeland" and breakaway from the ANC; 9 seats.

Independent Democrats: Led by Patricia de Lille, a former trade unionist and breakaway from the PAC, 7 seats.

African Christian Democratic Party: Aims to represent Christians in Parliament; 6 seats.

Freedom Front Plus: Established by staunch Afrikaners wanting to work within the new system; 4 seats.

Pan Africanist Congress: Another ANC breakaway, promoting the return of land to Blacks; 3 seats.

United Christian Democratic Party: Formed in former "homeland" of Bophuthatswana; 3 seats.

Minority Front: Party generally representing Indian interests; 2 seats.

Azanian Peoples' Organization: Espousing Black emancipation and Black consciousness; 1 seat.

The South African Communist Party has several MPs in the Assembly, but they are all appointed by the ANC. There are also several members of the SACP in the ANC Cabinet. The leader of the Opposition in the General Assembly is Tony Leon, of the Democratic Alliance.

Chief Justice Pius Langa and his judges head the judiciary. Judges are appointed by the President in consultation with the Judicial Service Commission, the leaders of the political parties represented in the National Assembly and, if relevant, the President of the Constitutional Court. There is a Constitutional Court, the highest in the land, as well as Appeal and Supreme Courts, and a range of courts below them. The common law of South Africa is Roman–Dutch Law, which is derived from the seventeenth-century law of the Netherlands, which in turn had developed from Roman law.

...AND POLITICS

The political scene in South Africa is dominated by the ANC, which used the Freedom Charter of 1955 as its basic policy document. Many of the tenets of the Charter are obvious policy choices: "The people shall govern; All national groups shall have equal rights; The people shall share in the country's wealth; The land shall be shared among those who work it; There shall be work and security; The doors of learning and of culture shall be open; There shall be houses, security and comfort."

In 1994 the government adopted the Reconstruction and Development Program (the RDP), which has four basic tenets: providing people's basic needs, such as housing, water, and electricity; developing the country's human resources; building the economy; and democratizing state institutions and society. It also adopted GEAR— Growth, Employment, and Redistribution—as a macroeconomic policy, or a strategy for achieving the RDP.

Much has been achieved. By 2004 some 78 percent of South Africans had their own homes, up from 64 percent in 1994, but the housing backlog remains severe, with millions still lacking formal housing; 85 percent had access to electricity, up from 58 percent in 1994; 75 percent had access to water, up from 68 percent in 1994, and there is a basic free water allowance for all households; 80 percent of the population is functionally literate, up from 66 percent in 1994 (expenditure on education is the single biggest budgetary item, up to R70 billion in 2003), and the number of beneficiaries of social grants had reached nearly 8 million at a cost of over R37 billion.

Political hot potatoes remain issues such as land reform, HIV/AIDS, corruption, crime, the provision of services, and unemployment. All these issues tend to be interrelated, making them all the more difficult to resolve.

Land Reform

Land, this most primary of all natural resources, has been an issue for two thousand years. There has always been disputed ownership of land. The original inhabitants, the San, believed no one could own the land, then the KhoiKhoi and later the Blacks arrived and needed land for their cattle, and then, of course, came the Whites. Land remains perhaps the most contentious issue today. There have been nearly 80,000 official land claims since the mid-1990s, ranging from individual private residences or businesses to farms and other areas covering hundreds of thousands of hectares. So far a little over half the claims have been settled at a cost of R1.9 billion (up to 2004). There is a long way to go, however, and there is much dissatisfaction, but the government has steadfastly declared that it will never allow the Zimbabwe landgrab situation to develop in South Africa.

HIV/AIDS

More than 10 percent of South Africans are HIV-infected, the country being one of the worst affected in the world. The pandemic affects every sphere of society, and the cost is astronomical. The eventual effect of AIDS deaths on the national economy and social life is incalculable.

Corruption

This is an issue that affects everyone, both the good guys and the bad guys, from the lowliest citizen to almost the highest in the land. The government has launched campaign after campaign against it, but the problem remains both acute and chronic.

Crime

South Africa's crime rate is one of the highest in the world, particularly as far as crimes of violence are concerned. This may not be surprising, given the country's violent past, but it is still bad news for all South Africans, and for visitors. The government says it is trying, but what is required is a change in mind-set among ordinary people, that crime is wrong and does not pay.

Provision of Services

Despite the government's achievements, there have always been heightened expectations in this area because of years of promises. There have been violent responses, including civil unrest, to what is a very real problem, or even sometimes a perceived problem. Some of the services highlighted are housing, water, electricity, and even toilets.

Unemployment
See page 43, below.

THE ECONOMY
South Africa is rich in natural resources, particularly minerals and physical beauty. The

minerals mean that mining and manufacturing are important, but so also is agriculture, and tourism is increasing, becoming a major economic factor. With its natural and human resources, South Africa has been for decades the economic powerhouse of Africa.

South Africa's is a free market economy. At more than R1,219,000 million, South Africa's gross domestic product (GDP) is the largest in Africa, taking up 25 percent of the continent's GDP, and the country's economy is considered to be the twelfth-most resilient in the world. The

economy has shown an upward trend since 1999,
the longest period of economic expansion in the
country's recorded history. During this period the
annual economic growth rate averaged 3.5
percent (up to 2005). The consumer inflation rate
has been showing a downward trend, averaging
4.3 percent in 2004. The International Monetary
Fund (IMF) has given South African economic
policies its full support, stating that they have
resulted in strong growth, low inflation, good
fiscal policy management, and a marked increase
in foreign reserves, and all of this has had a
positive impact on the rest of the continent. The
country's international credit rating is high
because of the economy's performance and
entrenched macro-economic stability. The
Johannesburg Securities Exchange (JSE) is one of
the twelve largest stock exchanges in the world.

South Africa has a modern infrastructure, including sophisticated financial and transportation systems, low cost (possibly the lowest in the world), and widely available energy (created largely from coal with a tiny nuclear input), sophisticated telecommunications systems, natural mineral and metal resources, a growing manufacturing sector, and strong growth potential in the tourism, higher beneficiation (added value to raw materials), manufacturing, and service industries.

There is a strong trade union movement, and it must be born in mind that COSATU is a member of the tripartite group that is the government. There are frequent strikes and what is known as "rolling mass action," often turning destructive and violent.

Unemployment is one of the most serious problems facing the government. Depending on whom you believe, the rate ranges from 25 percent to over 40 percent, with a heavy leaning of opinion toward the latter. This clearly has a negative impact not only on the economy and poverty levels, but also on the crime situation. It is said that between 30,000 and 40,000 new jobs are being created every month, but that is basically absorbing school graduates and needs to be virtually doubled if any real dent is to be made in the problem caused by the burgeoning population. The importance of a job is emphasized by the average ratio of one worker to ten dependants.

The main cause of unemployment is a lack of skills at just about every level, and although there are many training programs in operation there are evidently not enough. Mechanization is another problem—as wages go up, so does mechanization. Cheap imports (mainly from China) are yet another problem, causing the closure of factories, particularly clothing factories.

SOUTH AFRICA IN AFRICA

South Africa has assumed a leading role on the African continent. It has held a leading economic position for decades, but now that has been expanded to cover the diplomatic field as well. Apart from the areas already mentioned, on the economic front South Africa is a major sponsor of and heavily involved in the New Partnership for Africa's Development, a cooperative effort to do something about the continent's grinding poverty. On the diplomatic or political front, South Africa has been a major backer of the new African Union (the AU, established in Durban in July

2002), successor to the less-than-successful Organisation of African Unity. South Africans have also been involved in major efforts to negotiate peace in both West Africa and in the Great Lakes region, including the Democratic Republic of the Congo, and South African peacekeeping forces have seen action in several countries including the Congo (DRC), Burundi, Sudan, and the Ivory Coast.

chapter two

VALUES & ATTITUDES

THE NEW SOUTH AFRICA

It was described as a "miracle." South Africa, a country that the international community had almost willed to implode, had made the transition from Apartheid to democracy, not without loss of life and major stress, but it had made it nonetheless.

There are without doubt tensions in the new South African society, but the democracy holds and the country is stable. People get along remarkably well, far better than one could possibly have imagined before the transition, although, of course, the transition is still very much in progress. Attitudes have doubtless changed. There are still diehard racists in every community, but their voices are muted and generally South Africans are learning to live together. There is a race card, which is hauled out when people feel "put upon," a hint of "reverse Apartheid," as it is known locally, but by and large the society is functioning as well as can be expected.

This did not happen by accident: a lot of effort was put in to make South Africa work, including some much-needed unifying symbols. So, Nelson Mandela, who was already on the stage, was joined by the flag and the national anthem.

UNIFYING SYMBOLS

In a country of such diversity, unifying symbols are clearly of great importance. There was much uncertainty in many communities about the future of the country when in February 1990 President F. W. de Klerk announced the lifting of the ban on the ANC and the release of political prisoners, including the most famous of them all, Nelson Mandela. Nelson Rolihlahla Mandela, now affectionately known as Madiba by virtually all South Africans (*Madiba* basically  means, respectfully, "Old Man," but it is also the name of his Xhosa clan), had been in prison for twenty-seven years. He had been convicted at the Rivonia Treason Trial that ended in 1964. However, instead of an embittered old man and politician bent on revenge, there emerged a man who was bent on reconciliation, a man to whom all South Africans warmed almost immediately.

Madiba has become the Grand Old Man of
African statesmanship, and is universally
recognized as the father of the new South Africa.

Meeting Madiba . . .

It was at the Johannesburg Press Club's
Newsmaker of the Decade banquet. Madiba,
obviously the recipient, was leaving, when he
suddenly broke through the tight circle of security
men and officials and headed straight in my
direction. Now, with my long(ish) grey hair and
white beard I look rather like one of the Afrikaner
patriarchs of old, even in a dress suit, and the
beard tends to hide my grin. All Madiba had seen
across that very crowded room was someone he
imagined needed converting, and he accepted the
challenge. He arrived at our applauding table with
a jet stream of nervous followers, reached out a
hand to me, and said, *"Jy lyk baie kwaad!"* ("You
look very cross," in Afrikaans). I was too surprised
to react with the sort of aplomb we all dream of,
but muttered something about being pleased to
meet him, introduced him to my wife, and he was
gone. But he need not have bothered: I, like most
people, was converted years ago. It shows, though,
the measure of the man, that one face in a crowd
will spark such a reconciliatory gesture.

The flag is another remarkably unifying symbol. It was born at a time when everyone feared the worst, just before the April 1994 elections. People were nervous, many stored emergency stocks of groceries, some hoarded drinking water or gasoline— these were often rather grimly described as "Mandela supplies." The nation needed a lift. The flag's birth was not an easy one; there was plenty of input, but there was plenty of rejection too. Eventually it fell to the chief negotiators of the National Party government and the ANC and the State Herald to sort it out. They did so, and the new flag was proclaimed on April 20, seven days before the election. Flag makers had seven days to get South Africa's new symbol up and flying, and they did it. There is apparently no serious symbolic meaning in the design or the colors, just a sense of convergence of many diverse elements working in unison (the red band is always at the top). The flag is now almost universally popular, seen painted on mud huts in rural settings, on faces at sports gatherings, and on backpacks and suitcases in remote corners of the world.

The national anthem was another difficult birth, but what emerged was a clever compromise that was typical of many clever compromises that allowed the new nation to happen. The old White anthem, *Die Stem van Suid-Afrika*, "The Call of South Africa," was incorporated into an African hymn or song of praise, *Nkosi Sikilel' iAfrika*, "God Bless Africa," composed in 1897 by Enoch Sontonga, a South African Methodist schoolteacher. It has been accepted by virtually all South Africans, of all races, and is sung on all appropriate occasions.

"PROUDLY SOUTH AFRICAN"

There is a campaign, called "Proudly South African," aimed at promoting South African companies, products, and services that are helping to create much-needed jobs and economic growth in the country. Proudly South African is not, as it might seem, jingoistic, but rather a genuine pride in things South African. The campaign is supported by organized labor, organized business, government, and community groups, and is a way for all South Africans to contribute to the building of the nation. People or companies who meet the standards of the movement may use the Proudly South African logo, thus promoting themselves, their products,

and their services. It really works, too. Banks and
village craftsmen and women belong, fish and
chip shops and newspapers belong, schools and
fire stations belong, and the Drakensberg Boys'
Choir belongs.

South Africans of all backgrounds are justifiably
proud of what this new nation has achieved. It is a
marked attitude that visitors cannot help but
notice. In the old days there was a certain cynicism
to the question, "So what do you think of South
Africa?" usually asked of someone who had been
in the country for less than an hour, because in the
old days everyone seemed to be an expert on
South Africa and its problems. Today, the question
is far more likely to be genuine and based on an
obvious pride in the country.

Of course there are still cynics, and well there
might be because all is not perfect, but things are a
lot better than they could have been. Many people
still talk about Apartheid (foreigners usually
mispronounce it—it should be pronounced
"apart-hate," not, "apart-height"), but the truth is
that by far the biggest age group of South Africans,
those below the age of fifteen (a third of the total
population), never actually knew it. And the rest?
Well, of the older two-thirds of the population
many still revel in the freedom, many are
disillusioned (note the civil unrest in recent times,
aimed primarily at poor service delivery and

municipal border disputes, but still reminiscent of
the bad old days of the 1980s), and a few still live
in the past—but then there are those in every
society who live in the past. Still, there are more
cries of "Viva!" than there are of "Shame!"

The nature of Proudly South African, of
patriotism, has changed in South Africa. There
was a time when people were proud to be South
African, but they might also have been more
proud to be a Black, or an Afrikaner, or a member
of any of the other many groups. Today, Black
South Africans are overtly proud to be African, by
which is meant a citizen of the continent, then
proudly South African, then proudly Zulu, Xhosa,
or Swazi. The same can be said for just about
everyone else. Those unifying symbols have
generally done their work, and South Africans
now tend to be South Africans first, then proud
members of their own community.

UBUNTU

Ubuntu is an ageless African concept basically
standing for kindness toward other human
beings, for caring, sharing, and being in harmony
with all of creation. For the individual it means
something like, "I am what I am because of who
we all are." In Zulu, for *ubuntu* is a Zulu word, this
is, "*Umuntu ngumuntu ngabant.*" As an ideal, it

promotes cooperation between individuals, cultures, and nations, an ideal founded on the concepts of unity, collective work and responsibility, and empowerment through discipline and common purpose. President Thabo Mbeki has said, "There is no doubt that we are a diverse society, but all of us have consistently urged that we use this diversity as a strength to unite our people. Within this society are dominant values that bind communities together and ensure social cohesion. These values drive communities to act in solidarity with the weak and the poor, and help community members behave in a particular way for the common good. African people in this country have over centuries evolved a value system of *ubuntu*, with its basic tenet *motho ke motho ka batho ba bang* [a person is a person through other people]. Many of us have been brought up to uphold values based on this old African adage."

That great South African sage Credo Vusamazulu Mutwa, in his book *Isilwane—The Animal*, touches upon the difference between *ubuntu* and Western thinking when he says, "Under Western civilisation, we live in a strange world of separatism; a world in which things that really belong together and which ought to be seen as part of a greater whole are cruelly separated. The result of this separatist attitude is that humanity is denied a great deal of valuable knowledge. We are led into a forest of confusion when we try to learn about ourselves, our mother, the Earth, and the universe of which our planet is an infinitesimal part."

An example of *ubuntu* is ex-President Nelson Mandela's once giving a third of his salary to the Nelson Mandela Children's Fund, which he had established to help underprivileged children in South Africa. Another example is how the one person in a family or group with a job, even the most menial of jobs, will willingly support all the others (discussed under Work and Money). This is a very "African" thing.

WOMEN TO THE FORE

The issue of women in African society is a difficult one. It would be safe to say that in an earlier time and in a tribal situation, African women would have

stayed at home, looked after the homestead, the family, and the crops (the young boys looked after the cattle), while the men made war or hunted and waited for war. In many rural communities little has changed, however, except that the men no longer go off to war, but rather go off to work in the cities, coming home periodically with the benefits.

There are exceptions, of course (like the Modjadji, the Rain Queen of the Lobedu people of northern South Africa), but traditional African societies tend to be patriarchal. This means that the king, the chiefs, the subchiefs, and the heads of families, in that order, are in authority. Men have authority over women, older people over younger people, brothers over sisters of the same age or younger. The key word is authority. Remember that part of South Africa's system of government is the House of Traditional Leaders, a consultative body, so the system has been taken into account even in a modern governmental setting.

SUPPER WITH THE KING

We were invited, my wife and I, down to KwaZulu–Natal with a small group of people presenting King Goodwill Zwelithini kaBekiZulu with a pair of Blue Cranes, the Zulu national bird (only the King may wear its long tail feathers in his headdress, a tradition going back to Shaka, nearly 200 years ago). It was a very long ceremony at one of the royal residences, with praise singers, dancers, and drummers, where the King said, "We believe in traditions—tradition gives people their identity, and in these days when so many others are trying their best to destroy time-honored concepts for the sake of replacing them with nothing but ashes, we Zulus strengthen our traditions and customs even more."

Eventually the crowds departed and our group was left. We were invited into the King's lounge for tea. Later folding doors opened to the dining room, and we were invited to join him for supper. It was a most interesting meal, informal, yet traditional too. The King was addressed as "Your Majesty" throughout and he was served and waited on personally by one of his wives in the respectful way of the royal household. We had been immersed in Zulu tradition all day, and it ended with me interviewing the King on those traditions, including blue cranes.

In politics, across the cultural board, South Africa tends to have been a male-dominated society. There have obviously been some outstanding women in public life, but they have been few and far between. This, however, is changing. Today, South Africa is ranked eighth in the world in the number of women it has in government. The Deputy President is a woman, as are nine out of the twenty-seven cabinet ministers, eight out of fourteen deputy ministers, 30 percent of all members of parliament, and the Speaker of the National Assembly.

The Parliamentary Joint Committee on the Quality of Life and Status of Women has passed several pieces of legislation on customary or traditional law, domestic violence, and child maintenance. The Commission on Gender Equality (a statutory body set up to advance women's rights) has said, however, that while there may be good legislation and good policies, sufficient funding is required to ensure their proper implementation.

Women are also advancing in business in South Africa. Internationally, according to a survey, the country has the third-highest proportion of companies in which women are senior managers; in other words, 75 percent of businesses in South Africa employ women in senior management positions. As an example, the Johannesburg Securities Exchange is the fourteenth-biggest exchange in the world, trading over R1.3 billion a day, and since 2002 its Deputy CEO has been a woman, Nicky Newton-King.

Women have certainly come a long way in the new South Africa, but attitudes need to change still further. Some pressing problems remain, such as domestic and sexual violence against women; despite the advances, there is still a "glass ceiling" for many women in business; and in the more traditional setting women are often still not treated as equal partners in life.

THE SPIRIT OF ENTERPRISE

The rate of unemployment obviously has much to do with attitudes to work and money. As we shall see, there are two economic sectors in South Africa—a formal one, which is the conventional one, and the informal one, which is, on the face of it, less obvious. The informal sector is vital, and growing. It gives all people who would otherwise have absolutely no chance of getting a job in the formal sector an opportunity to make an honest living (unless you count often not paying taxes dishonest!).

For example, there is the street economy. You will find them on the manicured sidewalks of smart shopping streets, in the parking lots of suburban shopping areas, and on the dusty streets of townships and rural towns. These are the vendors, the informal purveyors of goods and services. They will be selling Asian knockoffs, anything from Nikes to Rolexes, for just a few rands. They will be selling local crafts that they have usually made themselves, such as pottery, baskets, grass mats, or wooden utensils. There will be the fruit and vegetable sellers, known as the "one-rand man [or woman]," who sell a neat pyramid of tomatoes, potatoes, onions, or bananas, or single apples or

oranges, for a fixed sum—though now this is likely to be two or five rands.

There are also the informal service providers, such as barbers. They will set up anywhere where there is space to position a chair, usually facing the passing show and the traffic, with a small gasoline generator for the clippers, and they are in business. Such a haircut may not be the latest style from London or New York (although if you bring a photograph of one of those they might have a go at it!), but it will certainly be a fraction of the cost. There are shoe cleaners, there are seamstresses and tailors working at treadle Singer sewing machines, there are cobblers, and there are appliance repairmen. In fact, you will find just about everything you need on the streets and sidewalks of South Africa. This is the entrepreneurial spirit at its best, in people who are making their own way.

It must be pointed out that, in a worst-case scenario, the generally accepted proportion of worker to dependant is one to ten. This means that everyone shining shoes or washing cars may be supporting ten people at home. This is likely to be a three-generation extended family, and is an example of *ubuntu* at work.

THE NON-CONTRIBUTORS

There are, of course, other, less positive attitudes to work and money. The unemployment rate and the level of crime cannot be separated, and there are those who have clearly chosen crime as a career option. Their attitude is obvious. There are also those who believe that the state is there to provide. There is a comprehensive social grant system in South Africa, including old-age pensions, child grants, and disability grants, and some nine million people benefit directly from the system. It's literally a lifesaver in some communities, where an old-age pension or a disability grant may support an entire family.

There are other situations, though, where some very imaginative ways are used to exploit the system. Long-deceased retirees still drawing their pensions years later are not unknown, nor is trying to have one's date of birth changed on an identity document so that one can draw the old-age pension early, and it is said that some women and teenage girls have had babies deliberately to take advantage of the child grant.

ATTITUDES TO FOREIGNERS

There are some very mixed feelings toward foreigners. It is certainly true that most foreigners are welcome, and that includes tourists and travelers, businesspeople, and immigrants on government-backed schemes. Tourism is rapidly outstripping other economic sectors in becoming a major creator of jobs and opportunities, and therefore tourists and travelers represent good business sense (this is not to say that South Africans are not naturally hospitable anyway). Businesspeople bring investment and opportunities into an economy that is in need of foreign input, and immigrants are needed to fill those positions that are locally unfillable because of a skills shortage. There are also craftsmen and women and artists who come to South Africa from other parts of the continent who seem to have no problem peddling their arts and crafts in street markets and informal "galleries."

However, it is the *Kwerekwere* who are unwelcome. These are foreigners from elsewhere in Africa who come into the country in droves, largely illegally, to seek work. There have been some very ugly instances of xenophobia, and the locals' attitude toward them is generally not good. It is a difficult situation. These are usually people who are desperately seeking a means to make a living, and if they do, send most of their income home to their families. They are often popular with employers, because they don't complain, are not members of trade unions, and will usually work for lower wages than South Africans. They are, however, often taking work away from South Africans, or are perceived to be doing so, and that is a problem. The government has massive schemes whereby these *Kwerekwere* are rounded up in the hundreds, kept in special centers to be processed, and then sent back across the border to their home countries. Often, sadly, they simply walk back across the dry riverbed and the whole process begins again.

Another issue is the drug dealers and organized crime bosses from certain African countries who use South Africa as a home base. The police are constantly breaking up drug rings and crime cartels, but there always seem to be more to fill the gap.

The other side of the coin is that there are many academics and perfectly legitimate businessmen from elsewhere in Africa who are not only welcome, but much sought after as valued contributors to the new South Africa.

chapter **three**

BELIEFS, CUSTOMS, & TRADITIONS

Every section in this chapter cries out, "Rainbow!" In religion, in weddings, festivals, feast days, high days, and national holidays, there is a wonderful variety of beliefs, of happenings, of ways of celebrating . . . read on!

RELIGIOUS DIVERSITY

Freedom of religion is guaranteed by the South African constitution, and Christianity, Islam, Hinduism, Judaism, Buddhism, Hare Krishna, and Baha'i are represented in South Africa alongside indigenous and traditional African belief systems, and mixtures of these with the major religions, especially Christianity. It seems that religion has always been important to the peoples of South Africa. From the first South Africans, the San or Bushmen, who believed in Higher Beings who took various forms and managed a spirit world linked closely to the animal world to which the San were inexorably linked as hunter-gatherers, to the many and varied forms of modern or traditional worship found across the country today, religion was, and remains, an essential part of life.

About 80 percent of South Africans are Christians, most of them Protestants, and many of them are with traditional African or Afrikaans Churches. The Church of Zion is the most important grouping of the African Churches. These Churches are primarily Apostolic or Pentecostal (a result of American missionary work a hundred years ago), so-called charismatic movements where the emphasis is on spirit baptism, faith healing, and speaking in tongues. There are many hundreds of these Churches, the largest being the Zion Christian Church (ZCC, formed in 1910) and the Nazareth Baptist Church, which have millions of adherents. Many of the followers wear bright uniforms (often blue or green and white) and may be seen with their drums and staffs in Sunday sessions in city suburbs. Many Christians also follow the traditional African belief systems, effectively combining the two.

The Afrikaans Churches have their origins in the Reformed Church, the first Church at the Dutch Cape in the seventeenth century. The Church evolved over the centuries, particularly after the British takeover of the Cape in the early nineteenth century, when the breakaway *Nederduitse Gereformeerde Kerk* (Dutch Reformed Church) was formed. The Church has undergone many reforms and changes since then, including the *Nederduitse Hervormde Kerk*, but the DRC and its many groupings are basically Calvinist in outlook.

The Roman Catholic Church, although not the majority Christian grouping in South Africa, is nevertheless well represented. Also represented is the Eastern Orthodox Church in various forms, including Greek and Russian. Other Churches include Anglican, Methodist, Presbyterian, Lutheran, and Baptist, while there are also very popular evangelist Churches in the country.

Christian Churches played a significant role in the events leading up to the changeover in 1994, particularly the Anglican and Roman Catholic Churches, but also some notable clergy from the

Dutch Reformed Church. In fact, in recognition of this contribution, the Nobel Peace Prize Laureate and former Anglican Archbishop of Cape Town, Desmond Tutu, became the chairman of the Truth and Reconciliation Commission that did so much to ease the old South Africa into the new.

Of the Indian population, slightly more than half are Muslim and most of the rest Hindu. Of the Muslim population, the vast majority is Sunni, and there is a tiny minority of Shi'ites (the original Malay slaves and the indentured workers from India in 1860 were Sunnis). Mosques, many of them very beautiful traditional edifices, may be found in all major centers, but do not be surprised if you drive through a small country town and spot a characteristic onion dome on the outskirts. The golden-domed Grey Street Mosque in Durban is probably the country's best-known Muslim place of worship. Most of South Africa's Indian population may be found in and around Durban or scattered across KwaZulu–Natal, although as already indicated there are important communities across the country. A major Muslim population will be found among the Colored community in and around Cape Town. They are the descendants of the original Malay population, mainly slaves, who came to South Africa in the early years. There are also a number of Black African Muslims.

There are well-represented Hindu communities throughout South Africa, but obviously particularly in Durban and the rest of KwaZulu–Natal. There are traditional temples in many centers, the Umgeni Road Temple in Durban (Sri Vaithianatha Easvarar Alayam Temple) being the biggest and the oldest in the country, and there are also some modern and magnificent architectural confections, like the Temple of Light south of Durban. They are all usually open to the public. Hindu festivals are also usually open to the public—but more of that shortly.

There is a notable Buddhist center and temple to the east of Tshwane (Pretoria), but Buddhism remains a fringe religion in South Africa.

Like the places of worship of other minority religions in South Africa, synagogues will be found in all major centers and the Jewish community is a small, but significant one.

TRADITIONAL AFRICAN RELIGIOUS BELIEFS

In the context of the entire continent of Africa and its one billion people, there are vast differences between the belief systems of East, West, North, South, and Central Africa.

In South Africa, as indeed throughout much of sub-Saharan Africa, there is generally a firm belief in the power and importance of the ancestors. There are Higher Beings, but the way to approach them is through the ancestors. The Zulu, for example, have always had Umvelinqangi as the All Powerful One, the Xhosa have uDali, or Thixo, or Qamata, as he is also known. There are other, lesser beings, but it is the spirits of the ancestors (the Amadlozi or Amathongo to the Zulu) who

are the important ones. Many tribes believe that the spirits of their ancestors are their life guides, and they will look to them when important decisions need to be made. Just as the Higher Beings may only be approached through the spirits of the ancestors, so those spirits are usually approached through a diviner or medicine man (*isangoma* or *isinyanga*) as a mediator. Sometimes a sacrifice might be called for to rectify situations, if for example, a tribal taboo has been broken and the ancestors need to be appeased. The ritual of sacrifice is an important one and will be found at weddings and funerals, when a person is ill, or has recovered— in fact on just about any occasion. The sacrificial animal can be anything from an ox or cow to a chicken, and the sacrifice may take place anywhere, from rural *umuzi* (homestead), to township or suburban back garden.

Again, it must be remembered that many people who are practicing Christians still believe in the spirits of their ancestors.

An important part of the belief system (although not strictly religious), particularly of the Xhosa, is initiation, although it is by no means universal. Boys must submit to the *khwetha*, or circumcision. Initiation comes for both boys and girls, who are compelled to attend initiation schools. This can take up to three months of "survival" or life training, and during this time they will sometimes smear themselves with white clay. If you happen to see them in the *veld*, you must leave them alone, as they are not allowed contact with the outside world.

There is another side to these traditional beliefs, the *umthakathi*, the sorcerers or wizards, but the less said about these the better.

This is, by necessity, a very brief overview. This field of study is as broad as that of any of the world's major religions.

WEDDINGS

Pick a culture, pick a wedding. An African (Black) wedding may be tribal and traditional, or city and western, or any number of combinations in between. "White" European church weddings are more or less exactly that—all white froth, smart clothes, tiered cakes, first waltzes, and goings away, with a few local variations (the reception could be outdoors, the getaway car a 4 x 4). Muslim, Hindu, and Jewish weddings are likely to be traditional, and may be simple or lavish. The same could be said for weddings of immigrant cultures—but just add the outdoors factor. That factor could see some wonderful surprises—the ceremony on a beach, on a farmstead *stoep*, in a suburban garden, just anywhere outdoors. Those who officiate at weddings in South Africa are used to such requests. It is likely to be the African (Black) wedding that is going to be the surprise.

Now, where to start? A Black, traditional wedding, rural or urban (surprisingly, especially for suburban neighbors) could start with days of serious partying, not to mention negotiation. The main negotiation is over *lobola*, the bride price. This could run to perhaps ten head of cattle, even a horse, being paid by the groom and his family to the bride's father. Much of Africa had a cattle-based economy before the advent of modern economic systems and in many parts of the continent cattle are still king. A man's herd reflects his bank balance, his status, his level of success in life, as well as his spiritual and mental well-being. Cattle are a way of life, a vital part of the social system. They are there at birth, at death, and at weddings. Once the *lobola* has been settled, things swing into top gear. Traditional weddings are filled with spectacle and endless ritual. There are special costumes for everyone, there will be sacrifices and praise singing, there will be much drinking of home-brewed beer, there will be dancing and drumming, gifts will be exchanged, and vows will be made. There may be a symbolic war dance, and then more beer drinking. It could go on for three days, and much fun will be had by all, but the vows will be made and taken as seriously as those at any other wedding.

A Black urban wedding may be all or part of the above, including sacrifices and *lobola*, although that is as likely to be paid in cash as in kind. It may also follow the path of the full "white" wedding. An important feature of the many Black weddings (or most celebrations, for that matter) is that everyone is made welcome. This means that the guest list could swell from dozens to hundreds, causing a nightmare for the caterers, yet they always seem to cope.

An important point is that polygamy is practiced in some Black African cultures, although it is less common than it was.

FEAST DAYS AND FESTIVALS

These are as varied as the country's cultural and religious makeup. As is the case elsewhere, such feast days and festivals are for everyone, not just the official celebrants. Here are some of them, in alphabetical order.

Bierfests: Imitations of the famous German *Oktoberfest* are held in many places at any time of the year. They often involve homemade produce and crafts as well as the *bier und wurst* and oompah bands.

Boeredag, or Farmers' Day: Ad hoc festivities in rural areas, with open-air cooking competitions, *boeresport* (games like tug-of-war, tossing horseshoes, arm wrestling, and chasing greased pigs), local crafts and produce, which could include anything from wind-dried meat (*biltong*) to home-distilled fruit brandy (*mampoer*). Fire Alert! Don't drink and smoke at the same time!

Cape Minstrel Festival: Held over January 1 and 2 (sometimes referred to as *Tweedenuwejaar*—Second New Year), this is very much a Cape Malay and Colored community affair. Originally, in historical times, the Cape's slaves were given the second day of the year off, and they made the most of it. It has developed into a two-day festival of minstrel groups competing for top honors, rather like a Mardi Gras carnival.

Cherry Festival: Held in the eastern Free State town of Ficksburg each year in the season, usually in November—days of picking, eating, and drinking the fruit of the cherry tree.

Chinese New Year: Celebrated in the streets of South Africa's Chinatowns, or sometimes central venues, with fireworks, lion dances, food, and drink.

Christian holy days: Those celebrated include Easter and Christmas as general holidays, and other holy days as part of the Christian calendar.

Deepavali, or Diwali: The Hindu Festival of Lights, usually in October or November, celebrated with fireworks, street parades, music, food, and drink.

Eisteddfod: Held in the Gauteng town of Roodepoort every second year, this is an international festival of music, song, and dance, based on the well-known Welsh concept.

Flower Power: The arid region of Namaqualand in the Northern and Western Cape bursts into one of nature's most spectacular wildflower shows in spring—the timing depending on the rains.

Grahamstown Festival of the Arts: Held in July, this is a celebration of every artistic sphere of endeavor, with art and artists filling this cathedral town in the Eastern Cape.

Highland Gatherings: There are Caledonian Societies throughout South Africa, and such gatherings mean games, dance, pipe and drum competitions, and plenty of food and drink. They are usually held in winter. Apart from the gatherings, Burns Night (January 25) is celebrated in most major centers and in some remarkably remote and, to some, outlandish, places.

Burns in the Bush

The piper came out of the setting sun, through the thorn bush, playing "Scotland the Brave," as Africa sank into the red dust. The gathered throng, in full Highland regalia, or black tie, African traditional or best bush khakis, parted to let him through, and the game was on. We celebrated in the *boma*—we were in the middle of a heat wave, but the haggis was chilled—we had iced whiskey, roast turkey, and all the trimmings, and frosted Athol Brose. There was pipin' and dancin' and singin', and more iced whiskey. It was Burns in the Bush, in the Lapalala Wilderness of the Waterberg Mountains in Limpopo Province, January 2003.

Jacaranda Festival: Ironically, the jacaranda tree is an alien species, but its beauty in its flowering season is undeniable. The streets of the capital, Tshwane (Pretoria), are lined with jacaranda, and around September each year there is a huge street parade.

Jewish religious holidays: Such days are not really public affairs, although Jewish visitors may always join in with a local community.

Lusitoland Festival: This is an annual Portuguese "bash" held in Johannesburg, and a weeklong celebration of Portuguese culture including music, dance, song, and, of course, food and drink.

Muslim religious holidays: Visiting Muslims can join in with a local community. The month of Ramadan is well marked, as are the sighting of the New Moon and the celebration of Eid.

National Days: Some foreign communities have National Day celebrations, often at their own cultural clubs. These include Americans, French (there is an active Alliance Française), Germans, Greeks, Irish, and Italians.

Reed Dance or Ceremony: A Zulu tradition celebrating chastity, in which Zulu maidens dance with reeds before the tribal leaders.

Sardine Run: Every winter (June/July) a natural phenomenon occurs off the coast of southern KwaZulu–Natal that still has scientists guessing. Millions of sardines, followed by dolphins, sharks, seabirds, and anything else that eats sardines, mass up the coast, attracting just as many human predators on the shore.

Whale Festival: An annual event in September in the country's whale capital, Hermanus, on the

Cape South Coast. Arts and crafts, flower shows, food, drink, and whales!

Wine Festivals: In season, usually in the Cape wine lands, there are opportunities to sample your way around South Africa's famous wines.

NATIONAL AND OTHER HOLIDAYS

These are national public holidays, when work closes down and play stays open. Businesses, trades, and financial institutions will be closed, but all entertainments will be flourishing. South Africa has a lot of public holidays—more than most countries—and South Africans don't like to miss them, so if a public holiday falls on a Sunday, the following Monday will be a holiday. And South Africans really enjoy their long weekends. Even a three-day weekend will see major traffic arteries packed with vacationers streaming to the coast or inland resorts. Holidays that fall on a Tuesday or a Thursday may well turn into a four-day weekend for many people, as the intervening working day conveniently disappears. On days of some political significance, politicians will make speeches and there may be a rally or two, but for the vast majority of South Africans it is just a day off.

School holidays are another opportunity for

"time off." State schools have four terms, which means that there is a short break around the end of March or beginning of April, to rejuvenate the kids and get the parents on to the beach and the golf course. There is a long break toward the end of June and beginning of July, the July "hols"— this is an important winter break and the visitor should make a note of it. Inland provinces like Gauteng are generally emptied in the direction of coastal areas like KwaZulu–Natal with its semitropical, warmish winter climate, and this is not a good time to be looking for accommodation or peace and quiet.

The Festive Season Break is a national institution. Schools shut down at the beginning of December, industry closes down in the middle of the month, and thereafter nothing happens in South Africa until at least the middle of January. Inland cities like Johannesburg experience a month of bliss—there's no traffic, one's favorite restaurant has tables to spare, and the fever pitch of Joburg business turns into a snail's pace. No one is reachable on their telephones, recorded messages reign supreme—the nation is "out to lunch." The media call it *komkommertyd*—literally, cucumber time, when nothing happens. It's the silly season. No politician would dare have a crisis over the Christmas vacation, as nobody would listen, or read. On the other hand, the country's

beaches are at their best, the weather is generally superb, and South Africans are at their most laid-back. So, if you can put up with the crowds, the bikinis, the surf, and the barbecues, go for it!

PUBLIC HOLIDAYS
January 1: New Year's Day

New Year's Day is definitely a day for the open air. Those near the coast go the beach, those inland spend the day around the pool with a *braaivleis* or go out for a picnic.

The night before, however, New Year's Eve, is a very different picture. Many South Africans take it quite seriously. There are private parties and functions in all communities, many of them sophisticated affairs at which formally dressed people wearing paper hats cheer and sing (or at least hum) "Auld Lang Syne" at midnight. Others are not sophisticated. In many major cities crowds of revelers start gathering in certain areas quite early in the evening, and the police tend to start gathering as well. In places like Hillbrow in Johannesburg (once claimed to be the most densely populated suburb in the British Empire) things can get ugly. At midnight there will be the popping of corks, but out of high-rise windows and off balconies will be thrown television sets, microwave ovens, furniture, in fact whatever takes someone's fancy at the time. If you must see the action, wear a crash helmet; otherwise join one of the perfectly normal and joyous street celebrations or parties elsewhere. Fireworks are big in South Africa, although there are ongoing calls for them to be banned, and New Year's Eve is fireworks time. It's noisy. Also noisy is the traditional thumping of streetlight poles, in fact anything that will make a racket, and screams of, "Heppi, heppi!" (Happy New Year!).

March 21: Human Rights Day

This day commemorates the Sharpeville massacre on March 21, 1960, when the police fired on a crowd of about 20,000 people demonstrating against the pass laws around a police station near Vereeniging, south of Johannesburg. Sixty-nine were killed.

Good Friday

A high percentage of South Africans are Christians, and services are held in churches throughout the country.

Family Day

In deference to those who are not Christians, Easter Monday has become Family Day.

April 27: Freedom Day
This day marks the first democratic elections of 1994.

May 1: Workers' Day
This is the equivalent of May Day, or Labor Day, elsewhere in the world.

June 16: Youth Day
This day marks the beginning of the uprising by Soweto schoolchildren in 1976.

August 9: National Women's Day
This day marks the genuine national thrust toward gender equality.

September 24: Heritage Day
This day celebrates South Africa's cultural and natural heritage.

December 16: Day of Reconciliation
This is an interesting one. On this day in 1838, a commando of 464 *Voortrekker* men under the command of Andries Pretorius, hell-bent on revenge for the earlier massacre by King Dingaan of the Zulus of another *Voortrekker* leader, Piet Retief, and his followers, defeated a Zulu army of some 10,000 warriors at the Battle of Blood River. The *Voortrekkers* were in a well-defended laager of

wagons and managed to kill some three thousand Zulus, suffering just four men wounded themselves. The *Voortrekkers* took a vow before the battle that if they won, they would keep the day as a Sabbath for evermore. It became the Day of the Covenant, then in 1994 in another of those masterly moves under the new dispensation, the Day of Reconciliation.

December 25: Christmas Day

December 26: Day of Goodwill (Boxing Day)

In conclusion, South Africans are not really enthusiastic about street festivals in the way these may be experienced elsewhere in the world, although there are obviously exceptions to this, but they do know how to holiday and how to party. The visitor should have no difficulty in linking up with either kind of celebration!

chapter four

MEETING SOUTH AFRICANS

Generally speaking, you will find South
Africans friendly. Some countries and
cultures around the world appear quite
alien to the visitor, and making friends,
even meeting people, is difficult if not
impossible. This is not the case in South
Africa, where most people across the board
are fairly Westernized (this excludes many
Black African rural communities, of course), and
are quite easy to approach. This does not mean
you will always make bosom buddies on your first
meeting, but be patient and you may end up with
a lifelong friend or two.

As many friendships begin with a handshake, it
must be mentioned at the start that a rather
different handshake from the usual is often used
in Africa, particularly by Black Africans. It is in
three sections or moves. First, the hands meet in
the traditional handshake. Second, the palms slide
from pointing downwards to pointing upwards
until each hand can grasp the other's thumb.

Third, the palms slide back to a second conventional handshake. Do not initiate this gesture—allow the South African to do it.

THE TIME FACTOR

South Africa is on Greenwich Mean Time plus two hours. That sometimes means very little. Many people are punctual and stick to appointed times, but there is another time standard. Much of the country is on Standard African Time, or Soweto Time, which basically means Any Time. One may suggest that time is *not* always of the essence here. This is not meant critically—it is just a matter of fact. Of course, there are those exceptions, so when making an appointment, be punctual—it may turn out that the person you are meeting is right on time, or you may have to wait an hour or two, but *you* should be on time. Planes, trains, and buses tend to run on GMT+2, as does much top business, but the visitor may be surprised at what, or who, does not.

HOSPITALITY

South African hospitality is legendary, and you may well be invited back to people's homes. Clearly you can expect from different South Africans some very different homes. Indian South

Africans may usher you into Little Mumbai,
Hindu or Muslim, or just a very South African
home. Coloreds may do something similar,
particularly in Cape Town, where there is a large
Malay community. A White home will, apart from
a few local touches, be rather like any other home
of European origin. A Black home? Well, that will
depend on whether we are talking urban or rural,
but it is very likely to be similar in many ways to a
White home.

A small gift on arrival is a nice idea, a bottle of
wine (though not for a Muslim household), a
bunch of flowers, a box of chocolates, or, if you
think of it in advance and can come prepared,
something from your home country. You can bring
a six-pack of beer if you know it's an outdoor
party, but bear in mind that South Africans are
lager drinkers, and that it should be cold.

FOOD

Of course, home
entertaining can be
anything from breakfast to
brunch, lunch, afternoon
tea, sundowners, and/or
dinner. South African food
is very varied. Much of it is
spicy and sometimes hot;

remember the African chili (*peri peri*) is very popular across the board. Spicy foods will include traditional Eastern curries, Malay dishes like *bobotie* (minced lamb or beef, but never pork), *bredie* (stew), or pickled fish. You may also get *waterblommetjies*, water lilies, which are delicious when cooked in the Cape style.

Venison is a possibility in the season. This may be traditional antelope or warthog (very much like wild boar). Ostrich is becoming more and more popular as it is so healthy. All these are usually roasted, but may be cooked or served in a variety of ways, such as ostrich steak, smoked venison, and venison carpaccio.

In a traditional Afrikaans home, particularly in the country, you may be given a *bord kos*, literally, a plateful of food. This is likely to include *vleis, rys en patat* (meat, rice, and potatoes). You'll probably get pumpkin too, and other vegetables, tossed with butter and possibly cinnamon. Traditional Afrikaans food also includes *vetkoek* and *koeksusters*, both made from dough and deep-fried, the first with a savory filling, the second dipped in syrup or honey and sugar. The savory *vetkoek* has also become very much a Black African dish. A farm kitchen is also likely to come

up with homemade breads and
jams, and of course the chutneys
that are the Malay heritage.

In both the Afrikaans and the
African home *pap* is another
universal food. Maize porridge or
mieliepap is the staple diet of much of
the population. *Pap* comes in many
different guises, so expect it to be anything
from porridgelike (usually made for breakfast) to
stywepap (stiff and malleable like plasticine) or
curled into twists like *kitke* (*cholla*) bread. And
while you are in an African home, think also of
some local vegetables, like the calabash or gourd
(marrowlike) and *marog* (wild spinach in many
different forms). A traditional African meal may
well be a plate of *pap*, meat stew, and vegetables,
sometimes eaten with the hands. The ingredients
may be in separate bowls in the middle of the
table, but then there is a whole etiquette to eating
with your hands from communal bowls—check
with your hosts.

There are some other African specialties in the
food line, which you may or may not come across.
These include walkie-talkies (chicken feet and
heads) or eversmiling (boiled sheep's head). A
rather grim history lies behind *chakalaka* or
seshebo, another constant companion to African
food—a spicy mix of tomato, onions, green

peppers, garlic, and chili. It had its origins in prison, where inmates combined everything they had received from their visitors to make a sauce for their meager supper. Last but not least, the mopani worm—a caterpillar, the size of a little finger, that lives on the mopani tree. In African cuisine it is sun dried, then reconstituted for cooking, which could be in many different ways. It is an acquired taste, but the one that you are most likely to be asked to try. Be brave!

THE *BRAAI*

One of the few South African universalities is the *braai*, or barbecue. If you are invited to a South African home, be it in a township, a smart suburb, or on a farm, it may well be to a *braai*. The *braai*, or *braaivleis* (literally, "roast meat"), started out as the campfire dinner for the early pioneers. Today it is a way of life, a national pastime.

First, African time may apply, which means you could be invited for 12:00 noon or 12:30 p.m. for lunch, but you may not eat until 4:00 p.m., by which time you could have been plied with so much alcohol that lunch matters not at all. On the other hand, you would not want to miss a South African *braai*. There will be an open fire of wood or charcoal, on which will be a selection of meats including some or even all of the following: *boerewors* (literally, "farmer sausage" in Afrikaans, a coarse-ground, spicy sausage), ribs (pork, lamb, or beef, plain, smoked, or marinated), lamb chops (a must), pork chops, chicken (portions or whole and butterflied, or spatchcocked), *sosaties* (kebabs), and steak. There may also be some, to the visitor, oddities like *netvet* or *skilpaaie* (savories made from offal); in fact the *braai* is an experimental laboratory to the home chef. There will also be sauces and marinades, the individual *braai*-ers' secrets, which have brought peaceful men to blows. There may also be a *potjie*, a black iron pot of *potjiekos* on the coals giving off fine smells of an equally fine, spicy stew. When you arrive the men will be gathered around the fire talking politics, crime, or sports (or sauce and marinade recipes), and the women will be inside making the salads. Of course it is not always the same, but that is a fairly typical *braai*.

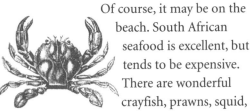

Of course, it may be on the beach. South African seafood is excellent, but tends to be expensive. There are wonderful crayfish, prawns, squid, octopus, mussels, oysters, and line fish. All of these go well on the *braai*, but they go equally well in the kitchen.

And while we are on universalities, there is *biltong*. This is spiced, marinated, wind-dried meat. It is as South African as the flag, and will certainly be found at as many sports meetings. It will also be at the *braai*, at sundowners, on the beach, and in fact just about anywhere.

Remember that many South Africans have swimming pools, and if you are invited for a informal lunch or just a lazy day, you may want to take along your swimming costume or bathing trunks just in case (it's a *cozzie* here, by the way).

In whichever home you eat, however, do not expect *cuisine minceur*. South Africans relish their food.

DRINK

South Africans have a reputation for enjoying the occasional drink. When it comes to meeting them all the usual norms apply—gin and tonic, whiskey and water or soda, a cold beer, possibly sherry, martini, or a cocktail (but less likely), then chilled dry white wine or red wine (often slightly chilled—when room temperature is 86°F [30°C], red wine goes into the fridge!). Also realize that there are some local specialties, like cane spirit, a white rum-type drink made from the abundant local sugarcane (usually drunk with mixers), and brandy—anything from the sort that you would only want to mix with cola (a favorite local drink), to fine after-dinner brandies. There is also the African phenomenon of sorghum beer, a home or commercial brew usually made from sorghum grain—a thickish, milky potion that the visiting palate finds is an acquired taste.

There is something of vital importance that must be said. The drinking and driving laws are draconian, the legal limit being 0.05 percent, and a zero tolerance approach is occasionally adopted. Many people now follow the international norm of having a designated driver, or simply calling a taxi. Don't take any chances. A night in prison could really spoil your visit.

Having said that, Cheers! *Gesondheid!* or *Khotso! Pula!* (a traditional Sesotho toast or greeting, meaning Peace! And rain!)

Sundowners

Sundowners are an old, ex-colonial tradition, established in tropical climes where the sun set at a reasonable hour and it was time to have a drink—at the end of a safari, a day's hunting, an afternoon of haggling in the bazaars, or just another day in the colonies. The drinks would hopefully be chilled, brought by a servant, and served on the veranda, the *stoep*, the deck, or perhaps around the beginnings of the evening fire in the bush. This is the time for gin and tonic, whiskey and soda, or ice-cold beer. It's a great tradition!

ENTERTAINING

If you are doing the entertaining, you have a number of options. You can meet to eat and drink out, or if you are self-catering you can entertain at your temporary home. If you decide to entertain at home, it's probably best not to attempt a *braai* yourself! A traditional meal from your own country is what would probably be most appreciated. Don't forget the drink, and if there is a good liquor store near you, you may even find some wine from your home country as well.

If you elect to eat out, which most people enjoy, you can of course choose the restaurant yourself, but you might do better to be guided by your guests, as there is a huge variety, from South

African and African traditional to the full range of international cuisine (see Chapter 6). Virtually all restaurants are licensed, but there are exceptions, so check. If they allow BYO (Bring Your Own), they may make a corkage charge.

"CULTURAL VILLAGES"

A cultural village is an establishment, a sort of model village, where indigenous people live out a typical traditional African life, often including nightlife, for the benefit of tourists who do not have the time or the inclination to seek out the real thing. There are many such villages, and they can be found in all provinces and near most major cities. For many visitors it is the easiest and most convenient way of meeting the locals on at least a superficial level, and can be highly recommended.

Such villages will usually allow you to experience the full spectrum of music, song, and dance, with good accompanying explanations of exactly how and why it is all happening. Just as importantly, it allows one an opportunity to try the local traditions of food and drink, also with explanations. You may be shown other aspects of the cultural life of Africa, such as a wedding, the arrival of a new baby, a funeral, or other special occasions in the tribal situation. And hopefully the whole business of traditional medicine and healing may be demonstrated—you may even have someone "throw the bones" for you (the reading of bones, shells, stones and other significant objects by an *isisangoma*) and have your fortune told (but be warned, do not trifle with such things).

Some cultural villages offer half-day outings, with a show and a meal, or overnighters where the visitor can get the full experience. There is one such village in Gauteng, for example, where four separate tribes are represented in four separate *kraals* (family units), so one may spend a night with a Zulu family, a night with a Xhosa family, and so on. This is probably the best option if you have the time, giving you an evening with your host family, a night in their home, and breakfast the next morning, with plenty of time for questions and answers.

Cultural villages may by their very nature be a little "touristy," but like similar features elsewhere in the world, they may be the best way of experiencing that all-important dip into Black African culture. If you want to observe the more contemporary way of life, you need to get yourself invited to someone's home or take a township tour.

FAMILY STAYS AND "B AND BS"

Another ideal way to meet South Africans is by staying in accommodation that is family-owned and -run. This comes in many forms, but the best would be guesthouses and bed and breakfast establishments ("B and Bs") where you are likely to meet and eat with the family. These could of course be urban or rural, but the rural stay may need a little more planning if you want to become involved in farming activities, for example. There are, for instance, B and Bs in the heart of tribal areas where you will experience not only "meeting and eating" with the family, but grinding the maize in the morning if you want a *vetkoek* for breakfast and milking a cow if you want a cup of tea with milk to wash it down! These are the ultimate homestays and cultural villages combined, giving you the best of both.

There is a useful organization for the traveler who wants to experience truly South African home hospitality in guesthouses across the country. This is the Guest House Association of SA (GHASA), which applies very strict standards and covers a wide variety of homes. Also always check with local tourist/hospitality/nature conservation authorities for local specials that do not always make it into the tourist books.

A LITTLE ETIQUETTE

The general sort of social etiquette that applies internationally usually applies in South Africa, but here are a few local specifics. If in doubt, however, ask.

Dress

Many South Africans, particularly in rural areas and across the ethnic board, are still fairly conservative. Cutaway shorts, tank tops, and similar revealing dress may offend. In apparent contrast, in cultural performances or in some tribal, rural situations you may well see bare-breasted women, but this is a purely cultural phenomenon and must not be misinterpreted as anything else. Ironically, at some cultural performances you may see women and girls wearing the full tribal regalia, plus white bras—this is a sign of the times. Remember that some religions, such as Islam, have dress codes of their own, and you are advised to respect this.

The Elderly

In many communities, particularly traditional
African ones, Afrikaner families, and many other
groups, there is great respect for the elderly. Spend
a little time with them, and if they indicate that
they are happy with this, there may be much to
learn. In Afrikaans, polite youngsters may well
refer to adults as *oom* or *tannie*, which mean
"uncle" and "aunt," but these are purely respectful
salutations. I was first called *oom* when I was a
teenager, and I was not impressed!

GREETINGS

There is a new custom when greeting many
Black South Africans. It can happen with
anyone—with the cashier in the supermarket
checkout, the man in the gas station, even the
waiter—and it goes something like this:

   The South African: "Hello, how are you?"
   You: "Hello, fine thanks, how are you?"
   The South African: "Fine thanks."

You may now get on with the business at
hand. Of course, you may initiate this
yourself, but the verbal ritual must be strictly
adhered to and completed.

Loud Voices

You may find that South Africans speak rather loudly. This happens even when two people are simply having an ordinary conversation, particularly at close quarters. It's a cultural thing.

Tribal Leaders

You may be introduced to a tribal leader. In many communities the head of the visitor (or anyone else for that matter) must never be higher than that of the leader. Follow the example of the people around you, and if you are in any doubt, ask. The rule is sometimes relaxed.

chapter five

SOUTH AFRICANS AT HOME

THE FAMILY

It is reasonably safe to say that the family is an important part of life to all South Africans, although that would be in varying levels of intensity and would take different forms. The extended family, comprising probably three generations living together as a unit, is the norm in many communities, but particularly in the Black rural community. In traditional rural areas the family will live in the homestead—a group of houses or huts. It will be close-knit, with the father/husband being the head of the homestead, and children living with the family until they marry.

The extended family living together is also common in other communities, including Afrikaners and Asian South Africans. In many Afrikaner homes *Oupa* and *Ouma* (Grandpa and Grandma) are still important members of the family.

Many people in communities across the board have tended to move toward the nuclear family of father, mother, and children. Young people move out of their parents' home and set up on their own, and when the time comes the older folk may move into retirement villages or other such institutions. The retirement village has become a distinct feature in the middle and upper echelons of the social landscape, with people moving into them at a relatively early age because they offer, among other things, companionship and security.

HUT TO HIGH-RISE

The South African home can be a grass hut, an apartment in a high-rise building in town, a large house in a leafy suburb, and much else besides. The grass beehive-shaped hut, a Zulu specialty, is rapidly disappearing, although one or two may still be found in rural homesteads, or *kraals*. One of the main reasons for the disappearance of these beautiful grass huts is the disappearance of the

building material. It takes four hundred staves or saplings to make a small Zulu hut, and four thousand for that of a chief, not to mention the thatching grass. The traditional mud and wattle, mud brick, or stone *rondawel* (round hut), or square hut with thatched roof, may still be found throughout much of the country. In a Black African homestead there may be several of these, ranging in size from one small unit for a single person to quite large houses.

In both town and country the more-or-less square, single-story brick house with a "tin" (corrugated iron) or tile roof is the norm for many communities. City suburbs and new housing estates or townships will comprise thousands upon thousands of these, costing, obviously, from perhaps R30,000 to millions, depending on the location, the size, the materials, the finishing, in fact everything. Such homes and their range could be virtually anything that you might find in any other country. Interior décor will be different from community to community, as will the nature of the surroundings, the garden, the street, and so on. The lower end of this market is likely to have been provided under a government housing scheme, and the rest is private enterprise, but basically this is suburbia for all communities.

There is a social phenomenon in South Africa that has kept pace with, in fact has probably overtaken, the rate of change in the country. Stretching back into the 1980s, Blacks have been positively shinning up the social ladder to form a growing and economically powerful middle class, and a growing and even more powerful elite. There have always been black millionaires in the townships, but now their numbers are increasing and they are often seen as setting the trend across the top end of the market (although many of them have remained loyal to their township roots).

At the upper end of the market there are obviously homes that reflect the wealth and lifestyles of that part of society. These again will differ according to individual tastes, and again they will reflect the international trends found anywhere else in the world.

Finally, there is one last housing sector, known as informal housing, or the squatter camps, to be found around and in the cities and many rural towns. These have come about largely due to the natural population increase and the phenomenon of urbanization. There has for years been a steady stream of people leaving their traditional homes in the countryside to seek employment in the cities, and perhaps the "bright lights" too. They seldom

find either, but at least in the informal settlements
they have each other. There are perhaps five
million people in hundreds of such settlements
across the country, and although the government
is clearly doing its best to correct the housing
shortage, it is just as clearly an uphill struggle.

LIFESTYLES
The lifestyles of South Africans vary enormously.
For most working people it is a five- or five-and-
a-half-day working week, with the weekends for
home and play. The eight- to eight-and-a-half-
hour day will be sometime between 7:30 a.m. and
5:00 p.m. Tradespeople tend to start early and
finish early, shops and offices a little later, and
shopping malls later still. For many people in
outlying residential areas the day starts really early
in order for them to get to work in the city on
time, and they get home late. Most use public
transportation and taxis; others use their own

cars. Lunch may be brought in a brown bag from home, or something in the work or office canteen, or a takeout. Supper is usually a family affair.

Television is probably the most popular home entertainment, and there are also DVDs and videos (there is a DVD/video store on almost every corner—DVD players are the fastest-selling household items in South Africa, and 19 percent of households have one).

For people in informal settlements the routine will be similar, but tougher. There are also those who are engaged in the informal sector of the economy, for whom there are no formal hours, also discussed elsewhere.

For those staying at home, particularly on weekends, sports are the important thing. At one end of the social scale golf is likely to be the pastime of choice, either for the club or the couch player in any community. There are those who watch rugby or cricket (fanatically, particularly among the Whites), or Wimbledon in season, or in fact any sport. Then there are those who watch soccer (football). Soccer is by far the most popular sport in South Africa—it is played by most and watched by most. The affairs of the national squad, Bafana Bafana (affectionately, "The Boys"), are a matter of public knowledge, not to

mention national pride (or not, depending on the latest goal scored). Soccer is played in multimillion-rand stadia, and on the street (particularly on the street!), but then so is cricket— neither keeps the kids off the street! And remember, South Africa will host the World Cup in 2010.

Internationally, South Africa has for many years perhaps been best known for its outstanding rugby and cricket teams and its golfers.

Weekends also see home entertaining (note the *braai*), work around the house, and gardening (more in some communities than in others). It's a

strange thing, gardening. You will find award-winning indigenous or European-style gardens in the middle class or in upmarket suburbs, but you will also find a few carefully tended flowers outside a mud hut way out in the countryside. Of course, you are also likely to find some maize growing around the hut, because many people grow their own vegetables and a little fruit.

South Africans also love the movies, and there are huge cinema complexes in the big malls, and individual movie houses in smaller places.

And then there is shopping. A visit to one of the world-class malls anywhere in South Africa at any time of the day, from Monday to Sunday, would give one the impression that South Africans are paid to shop and to sit at cafés drinking coffee. Of course, there is essential domestic shopping to be done, and that usually happens on weekends for working families, but the malls are strictly the territory of the young and the serious shopper.

EDUCATION

Education is a major thrust in the new South Africa, and the authorities are pouring considerable effort into it. There have been a number of dramatic changes in the educational system since 1994, from primary-school level through to institutions of higher learning. The current thrust is Curriculum 2005, and involves the frequently hotly debated system of Outcomes-based Education (OBE). OBE is a system where the concentration in the learning process is with the pupil taking the initiative, rather than the teacher teaching. It means a great reliance on the attitude of the child and on the study resources available to the child, and its success in South Africa still has to be proven (it has been tried in some other countries, like the United Kingdom and Australia, and not worked). One of the outcomes of OBE will be that the old matriculation (matric) examination (the equivalent of the North American Grade 12 Certificate) will become a thing of the past, and is being replaced by a Further Education and Training Certificate (FET). The FET will tend to move away from the purely academic qualification toward a more skills-based education, with the intention of improving the chances of getting that all-important job.

According to AMPS (All Media and Products Survey) figures, 93 percent of all South African children of the appropriate age are attending school (7 percent are apparently escaping, or missing, the education net and not going to school at all). Of that 93 percent, 83 percent are completing primary school and 35 percent are completing high school to matric level.

There are just fewer than 28,000 schools, a little over 1,000 of them independent or private. As far as the universities are concerned, there is currently a process in place to reduce the number of full universities by about one-third to about twenty-four, to rationalize and consolidate the higher education system.

As anywhere else in the world, school or university plays a major role in home life, with children being packed off to school in the mornings (schools usually open any time from 7:30 a.m. onward) and parents having to be involved in the usual extramural activities in the afternoons (schools close at around 2:30 p.m.). Note that you will frequently see children from all communities going to school barefoot. This is not necessarily a reflection of poverty (although it all too often is)—South African children sometimes go barefoot by choice.

And, for a final statistic to show that something in the education system is working, the basic literacy rate in South Africa now stands at 83 percent (2005).

THE MEDIA

Media freedom is guaranteed under the constitution, and there is a vibrant media scene in South Africa that is reflected in the use of the media at home. As already mentioned, television is probably the major source of entertainment in most South African homes. It is a fact that wherever electricity has been piped into an outlying community, it is the television set that has been the first family purchase to take advantage of it. There are three state TV stations, SABC 1, 2, and 3 (the South African Broadcasting Corporation, a giant in Africa), broadcasting news and views and general programming in most of the eleven official languages. There are of course both homegrown and American soaps, all popular viewing, but despite repeated campaigns to encourage or force the broadcasting of home-produced television, much of what is aired is American. There is an independent free-to-air TV station, E-TV, and then an independent pay channel, M-Net. There are also all the satellite networks available, such as Sky, BBC World, and Discovery.

Radio is even more broadly represented and is without doubt the most important and widely used of the mass media. There are scores of stations available, including the state broadcaster (SABC), commercial radio, community radio, local, and very local radio, in fact anything from shortwave to FM.

As far as the print media are concerned, every major city has at least two daily newspapers (a

total of twenty nationally, some of them having been around since the nineteenth century), and there are thirteen weeklies. Many households take a daily newspaper and the Sundays (mainly for the sports and the back page, which for many papers is strictly gossip and pin-ups), but newspapers are also bought and then swapped in the workplace. More than twelve million South Africans, a quarter of the population, buy newspapers on a regular basis. There are dozens of magazines covering every conceivable field of interest and for every population group and community.

And then there is the Internet. A growing number of South African families have access to a personal computer and therefore the Internet, and of course e-mail. It is estimated that 900,000 South Africans use the Internet every day, so this is something else that the locals are doing at home in their leisure time. From a true media point of view, an interesting South African phenomenon is Africa's first, and possibly still only, online newspaper. The *Mail&Guardian* has been on the South African media scene since 1985. A "thinking man's newspaper," it was at first harshly critical of the old regime, and today is still relentless in its pursuit of the right way of doing things. It is a bulky weekly, both in print form and online.

chapter six

TIME OUT

How much time South Africans have for leisure does not only depend on their economic circumstances. A squatter-camp resident with a gardening job may spend most of his waking hours working and commuting, but then so may a

top business executive. As we have seen in the previous chapter, if they have spare time they may spend it watching soccer or golf on television, or enjoying the Great Outdoors playing one of them. The Great Outdoors certainly features prominently in South African leisure time; from a quiet picnic for two, to a packed stadium full of sports fans, it is all "out there."

Before you step out in South Africa, however, be aware that many place-names across the country have changed. The administrative capital, Pretoria, is now Tshwane, although a few central city blocks are still officially called Pretoria. Johannesburg, the commercial hub of the country, if not the continent, has so far remained intact, although it is more often than not referred to as Joburg in the Old Speak and Jozi in New Speak. All airports were sensibly changed to the names of their mother cities (such as Johannesburg International Airport), but there is now pressure to change some of them again, after heroes of the new South Africa. You will find that cities, towns, and villages have changed their names, and so have highways, bridges, rivers, and the like. New road maps will have the new names, older ones may not, and not every South African knows the new names, so you may experience a degree of confusion when moving around the country and asking directions.

EATING OUT

South Africa's culinary tradition reflects its richness as a melting pot of cultures going back hundreds of years. You may dine at an ultra-sophisticated establishment with an ultra-high price tag, or you may buy a bunny chow to eat on a park bench (a bunny chow is half a loaf of bread filled with curry, wrapped in paper, and costing as little as R10—eating it is an extremely messy business, and takes some practice!). There are ethnic restaurants from all over the world, including Europe, Asia, and North and South America (including old favorites Cajun and

Creole, Brazilian, Indonesian, Malaysian, Thai, Vietnamese and Korean, Russian, Turkish, and even Californian). For a quick meal or solid and reliable victuals there are many local and internationally recognizable chain restaurants, from McDonald's and Kentucky Fried Chicken, to steakhouses like Spur and Steers, fish restaurants like Ocean Basket and The Fishmonger, and British pub look-alikes such as McGinty's and the Keg establishments. There is one other chain available in South Africa, the *Confrérie de la Chaîne des Rôtisseurs*, established by Louis IX in Paris in 1248, and today a worldwide association of member chefs, gourmets, and restaurants, an *Association Mondiale de la Gastronomie*, of which there are a number in South Africa. Selected restaurants that have played host to the *Chaîne* may carry its blazon and are therefore a fairly good bet. Remember that *Chaîne* status covers not just classical French cuisine, but gourmet fare from many other cultures too, including South African.

And then there is South African cuisine. This is clearly very varied, but the main categories would be traditional African (and that is not just from South Africa), Cape Malay, and Cape Dutch, regional Indian, and then a strong leaning toward Portuguese. Many of the dishes the visitor might expect have been described in Chapter 4, with the exception of Portuguese cuisine, which has become a big part of the South African scene along with the huge Portuguese community. The Portuguese are famous for their *peri peri*, the hot red chili of Africa, and this is well demonstrated in such dishes as the fiery but wonderful *peri peri* chicken or prawns. The Portuguese are renowned for their seafood dishes, so look out for their restaurants throughout the country.

On the subject of restaurants, for South African ethnic dining look for South African venues. You will find Cape Malay and Cape Dutch in abundance around Cape Town, and good Cape Dutch establishments in many other cities, including Johannesburg. Indian restaurants are ubiquitous, but particularly so in KwaZulu–Natal. For traditional African eating the townships are the place. Inquire of the local tourist authority or even at your hotel for day or evening tours to a township. The tours might cover many things, but ask specifically about eating and drinking and you'll almost certainly end up at one of the better-known taverns (as they are popularly known) or shebeens (as they were called in the days when they were illegal). Here you may eat and drink in safety, maybe listen to some African jazz, and even

spend a night. Be sure to take a tour, though—
don't attempt to undertake this independently.

This is a fickle business, however, and, as
anywhere in the world, a restaurant
recommended yesterday may be gone today.

...AND TO WASH IT ALL DOWN

Many South African wines are among the finest in
the world. The Western Cape, with its
Mediterranean climate, is by far the best wine
region in the country, although good wines are
also now coming out of drier regions like the
Northern Cape, with some excellent reds and
whites featuring prominently in international
wine shows. There are so many great vineyards,

winemakers, even
boutique producers,
that it would be
unfair to name
names, so ask your
waiter or wine
steward. There are
quite naturally also
some uniquely South
African spirits and aperitifs produced here too, as
well as fortified wines like sherries and ports
(names now in dispute with the European
Union). South Africa is particularly well-known

for its dessert wines, a tradition going back to the Dutch settlers, so ask about Malmsey, Marsala, Muscadel, and Jerepigo.

South Africa produces some fine brandies, and in the liqueur line there is the most famous, Van der Hum, with a tangerine flavor, then Amarula, made from the delicious fruit of the Marula tree, loved by humans and animals alike. Then there is mampoer, or *witblits* (white lightning), the fiery liquor originally distilled by the settlers from anything that would ferment, still often available (illegally) in the backcountry, but also distilled commercially (and legally!).

Napoleon's Favorite Wine

Some South African dessert wines have been world famous for centuries and one was even good enough for Napoleon Bonaparte. When exiled to the remote South Atlantic island of St. Helena after his final defeat at Waterloo, Napoleon was a lonely and sick man, but he took solace in *Vin de Constance*, a wine first made in Klein Constantia in the Cape some two hundred years ago. It was, and remains (for it is being made again and is still available) an excellent wine and may just have eased his solitude and the stomach cancer that eventually did for him what the combined armies of Europe could not.

DRINKING AND SMOKING

South Africa has draconian laws designed to control excessive drinking and smoking, but sadly this well-meaning legislation is not consistently applied or policed. Therefore you may transgress with impunity for some time, but if you are caught and have to suffer the consequences, don't blame the system. Generally, you may not drink alcohol in public, and that includes the beach. Alcohol may not be sold to people under the age of eighteen. The real crunch comes with driving. The legal limit is 0.05 percent, the same as in many other countries. If you overdo it (and it's difficult to say, but it could be no more than one or two drinks) and you are caught, it could mean a night in jail.

Smoking is illegal on public transportation and in most workplaces, public buildings (including airports), restaurants, and places of entertainment, in fact just about everywhere. Some locations, including restaurants, have dedicated smoking areas. Look around you before you light up, although seeing other people smoking may not be an indication that it is permitted. Tobacco may not be sold to people under the age of eighteen.

TIPPING

Given that First World/Third World situation again, if the traveler is in a First World situation such as a hotel, private taxi, or restaurant, it is safe to say that one would tip as one would tip at home, 10 percent being a reasonable rule of thumb. Airports and stations tend to have fixed-rate porters.

In a somewhat more informal or Third World situation, a small tip is appreciated for any service offered—a youngster opening a farm gate or helping with a flat tire on a country road. Given the unemployment rate, many people are trying to make a living by providing small services, particularly in the cities—car wash and car guard services are a good example. Many car guards in parking lots will be wearing some kind of uniform, for which they pay; they depend entirely on tips, so a rand or two will be appreciated. Gas station pump "jockies" also appreciate a tip.

If you are on an organized tour (coach, train, or bush safari) the situation is different and guides, trackers, and the like are going to get a lot more than small change. Check with the operator to see what is appropriate.

BEGGARS

Begging is a growing problem, and a very vexing one. You never know if the beggar is a slick operator making a good living in his or her preferred way, or a destitute individual to whom a couple of rands will make the difference between eating and not eating. The visitor may also be surprised to note that beggars come from all communities—poverty knows no neat pigeonholes. In South Africa begging is particularly noticeable at traffic lights, where you will find all sorts of people with signs hanging around their necks often giving highly imaginative reasons why you should make a *los* (contribution). There will be mothers with babies strapped to their backs with a blanket (a very traditional way of carrying a child, by the way) or with children playing on the traffic island, and there will be street children. You should know that special crèches have been set up for these mothers, but the babies are still being used as a begging prop, and there are shelters for the street children, but they just prefer the streets. The authorities are doing their best to discourage begging, so would prefer you not to encourage it.

SHOPPING FOR PLEASURE

The shopping in South Africa is excellent. There are huge, world-class malls with top-of-the-range shops and stores, restaurants, entertainment centers, and banking halls. There are supermarkets, ranging from the vast to the corner shop minimarket. The products in these shops, consumables and nonconsumables, come from every corner of the globe. South African fashion design is beginning to make its mark on the world's ramps, South African jewelry is doing the same, while arts and crafts, particularly African, are a must for every traveler to take home. Look out for basketwork, weaving, beadwork, pottery, and wire working (this is a local specialty, with anything from a Christmas tree to a soap dish being fashioned from ordinary fencing wire).

Remember that VAT paid by tourists on certain goods and services may be returned at the point of departure. Remember also that some items, such as skins, tusks, or bone, may be banned in your own country.

At the other end of the scale, don't forget the street economy—those vendors who operate on the sidewalks and who represent an important and very active sector of the overall economy. Support them if you can, as the system often eliminates the infamous middleman, with the income going straight to the vendor's family.

And then there is the *spaza* shop. This is an African institution. Usually run from a hole-in-the-wall, a garage, an old shipping container, or a side window of a township house, this is the ultimate convenience store, always just around the corner, carrying life's essentials: cigarettes and matches, candles, kerosene, bread and milk, canned fish, and *chakalaka*. You may even be able to buy (illegally) a cold beer.

Bargaining

Bargaining is generally not the everywhere, everyday norm in South Africa, but it is alive and well in one community. Indians seem to love to bargain, so one needs to play the game by their rules, and the rules are constant. Start by halving their first offer, and end up somewhere in between. By the way, this rule does not apply to the little spice emporiums and Indian food takeouts that you will find in many shopping centers and malls.

THE ARTS

The arts are very well represented in South Africa. Music across the spectrum may be found everywhere. All major cities have orchestras and therefore classical music performances, and the orchestras travel to smaller centers to give a broader reach. An exciting phenomenon on the music scene is the growing number of classical musicians, including youngsters, coming out of the townships, a trend that may have been set by the now famous Soweto Strings. Popular music there is aplenty, from folk, through rock and roll to township jazz; whatever it's called, you'll find it here. There are many fine musicians, composers, and recording artists too, from across the same spectrum, so take home lots of South African music.

Theater also ranges from the classical European repertoire to purely South African creations. There are full theaters in all major cities, of course, but theater will also be found at the local community level. Opera and ballet tend to be limited to the main centers, but here you will find full productions of the classics, and some experimental productions too. There are also some exceptional outdoor venues for theater and music.

Many even quite small towns have a museum, and of course there are major ones such as the South African Museum in Cape Town. There are art galleries everywhere, featuring international works of art, as well as local art and artifacts, and over the years South Africa has produced artists

who have exhibited internationally, such as
J. H. Pierneef, Irma Stern, Anton van Wouw,
Walter Battis, Gerard
Sekoto, and Norman
Catherine. The South
African National
Gallery in Cape Town
has a fine collection,
including works by
Gainsborough, Sir Thomas Lawrence, Frans
Hals, Pieter de Hooch, Anthony van Dyck, and
Louis Tocque.

South Africa has a long and impressive record
of contributions to English literature, including
writers like Olive Schreiner, Sarah Gertrude
Millin, Eugene Marais, Roy Campbell, William
Plomer, Laurens van der Post, and Dan Jacobson.
There have also been two South African Nobel
Laureates—J. M. Coetzee and Nadine Gordimer.

South Africa is becoming a center for
international film production because of its fine
weather, magnificent scenery, and an increasing
wealth of technical expertise. It is also becoming a
producer in its own right, with some homegrown
films reaping international awards. South Africans
love the movies, and there are huge cinema
complexes in the bigger shopping malls, and tiny,
old fashioned and charming cinemas in small
country towns too.

THE DISTANT PAST

It must not be forgotten that the latest scientific thinking puts the Cradle of Humankind right here in South Africa, just outside Johannesburg. Many of the world's most exciting archaeological and paleoanthropological sites are to be found here and many of them are open to the public, including the Cradle of Humankind site and Mapungubwe Hill on the Limpopo River in the far north. At the Cradle of Humankind is Maropeng, a visitor center that has won the British Guild of Travel Writers' Award for Best New Tourism Project Worldwide. It includes displays on geology, paleontology, paleoanthropology, and fossils, of course. It also has everything else you need for a day out in the past—it's well worth a visit to get in touch with your ultimate ancestors.

A combination of the arts and the distant past is the world-famous rock art of the San or Bushmen people, to be found throughout much of South Africa. Inquire locally for sites.

A SPORTING NATION

South Africans are without doubt a sports-mad nation. The big team sports, like football (soccer), rugby, and cricket, have a loyal following, both at matches and on television and radio, but there is also a loyal following for other sports, such as golf, tennis, and swimming. Remember that South Africa has over the years produced some of the world's greats, both teams and individuals, and the country is proud of that.

Attend a soccer match—it's a real South African experience (35,000 Zulus and 35,000 Xhosas shouting for their respective teams!), but make sure you go in an organized group, as it can get quite exuberant!

Some international household names in sports stadiums include Ellis Park, the Wanderers, King's Park, and Newlands. Adventure sports are also big in South Africa, and with its very varied terrain there is always room for action somewhere.

WILDLIFE, THE BIG GAME

The wildlife is the reason that many visitors come to South Africa. The experience may be a luxury private game reserve costing a small fortune, or a walk in a city nature reserve costing nothing.

There are many different levels of the wildlife experience between these extremes, and visitors must decide at which level they want to become involved. South Africa is one of the three most biologically diverse countries in the world (the others being Brazil and Indonesia), occupying less than 2 percent of the world's land space, yet having 10 percent of the planet's plants and 7 percent of its reptiles, birds, and mammals, so it's not just the Big Five (Lion, Leopard, Elephant, Rhino, and Buffalo). There are at least twenty National Parks representing all biomes, and hundreds of provincial, regional, local, and municipal parks. The parks range from the Kruger (as the Kruger National Park is known) to much smaller Big Five parks a short ride from the city limits, so the wildlife environment really is there for you. Of course, if you cannot make it to a game reserve, many cities have excellent zoos and bird parks too.

BEACHES, BEACHES, AND MORE BEACHES

Not a lot needs to be said about South Africa's famous beaches, and with around 1,900 miles (around 3,000 kilometers) of coastline there are plenty of them. There are lifeguards on the more popular beaches, particularly in the season, but others can be very lonely and therefore have a potential security problem—ask locally for advice. Be careful of treacherous bathing conditions too. South Africa's seas are the sharks' seas too, and although many popular beaches

 have shark nets, many don't. Again, check locally. On most beaches the usual rules apply—no alcohol and no vehicles—and there are local rules for local conditions.

GAMBLING

This has an interesting history in South Africa. Banned under the old regime because of Calvinistic principles, it always happened behind closed doors. Then came the homeland policy of creating "independent" states, here, there, and everywhere. These states immediately set up huge casinos and other gambling complexes, and the exodus into the homelands of South Africans in order to try their luck at the tables (usually after work or on weekends, as the casinos were always conveniently placed close to urban areas) became a feature of South African society. Of course, some people made a fortune, particularly the various governments involved (including South Africa's); most did not, however, but after 1994 the homelands disappeared and the casinos stayed. Today, South Africa's R36-billion casino industry has become one of the first outside the U.S.A. to bind itself to a code of conduct promoting a culture of responsible gambling. Of course there are also the horses and a couple of race days, including the Durban July at Greyville in Durban and the J & B Met at Kenilworth in Cape Town, have become national events, with just about every South African placing a bet or two. There is also a national Lotto, which has made many instant millionaires.

MONEY MATTERS

Most internationally recognized credit cards are accepted in South Africa, as are traveler's checks. Just keep a little money in your pocket for tips and street purchases. There are ATMs virtually everywhere, accepting both credit and bank cards—use them with caution (see Security).

chapter seven

TRAVEL, HEALTH, & SECURITY

DRIVING

This section should almost start with a
health warning. It needs to be said that
the standard of driving in South
Africa leaves much to be desired. All
the usual international rules of the road are in
place, but are regularly ignored, particularly by
minibus taxis. Perhaps it is sufficient to say that up
to 15,000 people die on the roads every year,
costing the country R38-billion annually, a
contributing factor being the possibility that a very
high percentage of driver's licenses are illegal or
invalid. Also note that more than half the accidents
on the roads are alcohol-related, and remember
those drunk-driving rules. Pedestrians walking on
the roads are a problem, and so are stray domestic
animals—be on constant alert for these,
everywhere. Driving is on the left, most of the time.

There are exceptions to the driving rule,
however. Long-distance truck drivers are usually
obliging and courteous (as indeed are many other

South African drivers), and will pull over to the left if you are trying to overtake them, for example. There is an interesting local ritual of courtesy indicator flashing. Flash once or twice to say "Thanks" for the pullover; the trucker will then flash headlights once in acknowledgment, and the overtaker may wave a final acknowledgment of the acknowledgment. A bit silly, perhaps, but a pleasant feature of the roads. (See Car Rental).

Cell phones in cars. It is illegal for the driver of a vehicle to use a cell phone without a hands-free kit. Despite what you will see around you, please don't do it.

PLANES, TRAINS, AND BUSES

South Africa probably has the most sophisticated nationwide transportation system in Africa. There are airports in all the main cities, airfields in smaller ones, and bush landing strips where they are needed. Apart from the national carrier, South African Airways, and its feeder services, there are a number of other airlines that fly nationally, providing a network of regular flights, including commuter flights, around the country, and then there are the bush pilots flying into remote and wonderful places.•

There are many suburban, regional, or commuter train services and mainline trains between all major centers. There are also a number of luxury train services, many of them world famous, which ply certain of the main routes, taking in some of the country's most spectacular attractions. These are more popular than the regular train services.

Also very popular with visitors are the many and excellent intercity bus services. These tend to be more convenient because they run from city center to city center, with many useful stops in between.

TAXIS

There are no cruising taxis in South African cities, but most cities have taxi services that will come and go as required. Taxis tend to be expensive. Less expensive are the minibus taxis seen everywhere throughout Africa, and although these are the most common form of public transportation on the continent, they are not recommended for the average tourist (see Driving).

GETTING AROUND TOWN

It must be accepted that public transportation in most South African cities is bad. There are no underground train systems, surface trains are commuter services rather than tourist ones, and bus services are similar. Take taxis.

CAR RENTAL

All the major international car rental companies are represented in South Africa, and the usual regulations apply. There are additionally local rental companies with the usual range of cars, but there is also an impressive range of 4 x 4 safari vehicles. Please remember that driving a 4 x 4 is not like driving a small car on a quiet country road. When you venture into Africa you need special skills with that safari vehicle; otherwise your vacation may be much longer than you had planned. A valid international driver's license is required, although some foreign licenses are also accepted. Gasoline or diesel costs around R7 a liter and is freely available. The country has the best road system in Africa, particularly the highways or toll routes (expensive, but excellent) and even the network of lesser and often dirt roads is usually good. As you would at home, check locally for local conditions. A cell phone is a good idea when driving, in case of breakdown or other emergency. As distances between comfort or fuel stops can be great, be prepared for that, and plan ahead.

Speed limits range from 25 mph (40 kph) in villages to a usual 37.5 mph (60 kph) in most urban situations, up to 50, 62.5, or 75 mph (80, 100, or 120 kph) on the open road or the highways. Beware of drinking and driving, as already mentioned, and watch your speed—there is punitive speed trapping. Also beware of road maps, in that place-names change overnight and not everyone, including the locals, may necessarily be aware of such changes. *Never* pick up hitchhikers. Drive cautiously and defensively, and enjoy the glorious scenery. If you do not want to drive at all, there are also chauffeur or driver/guide services available.

OVERNIGHTING

Much of the overnight accommodation scene has already been covered. Accommodation here ranges from a night in an international, the-same-as-home, luxury brand-name place that could cost you U.S. $1,000s (up to R10,000) for a bed, to a cot in a tribal bed-and-breakfast place for the price of a good bottle of local wine—take the tribal B and B (probably no wine available). There really is everything here, so take your choice, but remember that you have endless interesting possibilities—why sleep in a European four-poster when you can sleep in a Zulu grass hut?

GENERAL HEALTH

What goes for most countries goes for South Africa. One of the rare joys is that the tap water is drinkable almost everywhere. That means in hotels and the like, not so much very rural establishments, but most places, and where that is not the case there is a remarkable array of local (and international) bottled water. As a matter of interest, one local water authority bottled its water and gave it out free at highway tollbooths one festive season, and it was judged to be one of the best bottled waters in the country!

Check for any international health requirements. At the time of going to press, none are needed, but check well in advance of your trip and take medical advice. Watch out for malaria, which is a problem in the northern and eastern parts of the country. Don't take risks with it, as it can be fatal. Your doctor, chemist, or pharmacist will advise. You may also check Internet sites such as that for the Center for Disease Control in the U.S.A.

Mind the sun. It's the same sun as yours, but it can be more vicious over Africa. And mind nature—colonial tradition says, "Everything bites, stings, or scratches in Africa," and it probably does. Watch out for insects, reptiles, and, of course, the Big Five (Lion, Leopard, Elephant, Rhino and Buffalo).

If you need medical attention in South Africa, fall back on your international health insurance and find a private facility (there are parallel public/private facilities). Be particularly mindful of HIV/AIDS with needles, injections, transfusions, and the like.

South Africa has a major drug problem, both as user and as conduit. Don't get involved.

HIV/AIDS

South Africa has one of the highest HIV/AIDS rates in the world, which should ring warning bells for travelers. More than five million South Africans, 11 percent of the population, are infected with HIV and an estimated six million people are expected to die of AIDS-related diseases over the next ten years (340,000 died of AIDS and AIDS-related diseases between mid-2004 and mid-2005). The plight of AIDS orphans is a particularly harrowing one—one million households in the country are estimated to be headed by children, the parents having died of AIDS. The same health risk warnings and precautions apply in South Africa as would apply in your own country, except more so, so do not do here what you would not do at home. The government (although mixed messages

concerning HIV and AIDS continue to slip out)
has accelerated the "roll out" (politician-speak for
"distribution") of ARVs (anti-retroviral) and
myriad NGOs are doing sterling work in
combating the pandemic. There is an HIV/ AIDS
Helpline: 0800-012-322.

THE STATE OF SECURITY

There are many contributory factors to the
security situation in South Africa. Unemployment
is one of the main ones and, quite simply, the
history of the country is another. However, the
country's stable and growing economy should
eventually have a positive impact on the situation
and things should improve.

The crime situation is a matter of record. There
are about 20,000 murders a year, 55,000 reported
rapes (this is nowhere near the actual figure), and
so on and so on. There are estimated to be four
million illegal guns out there, and an AK-47 assault
rifle can be had for under R1,000 on the street. The
police are undermanned and outgunned, although
moves have been announced to change that.

Having said all this, however, you can spend
a perfectly wonderful holiday in South Africa
without having as much as a rude word thrown
at you.

POLICE HINTS AND TIPS

The South African Police Service issues periodic information sheets or pamphlets for both locals and visitors. The following points apply to visitors:

Personal Safety

• Know the police station number and all emergency numbers (10111 is for general emergencies. Look in the local telephone book for others).
• Always tell someone where you are going.
• Do not display valuables such as cash, credit cards, traveler's checks, cell phones, jewelry, or cameras in public.
• Never carry more cash than you need.
• It is better to explore in groups and to stick to well-lit, busy areas.
• If you are traveling with children be particularly watchful, as always.

At the Hotel

• Never leave your luggage unattended.
• Store valuables in the safe deposit box.
• Keep your room locked, whether you are in it or not, and check who is there before opening the door.
• Hand in your keys when you leave the hotel— never carry them with you.

In the Car

• Plan your route in advance and let someone know your plans.

- Keep car doors locked and windows closed at all times, particularly in towns.
- Be extra cautious when driving alone, especially at night.
- Park in well-lit areas at night.
- Avoid stopping at remote places (or at least be cautious, day or night).
- Never leave valuables unattended in the vehicle. Put them in the trunk (boot).
- Do not give lifts to strangers.

Safety while shopping
- Never leave valuable possessions in a cart or trolley.
- Don't allow children into a public toilet on their own.

Safety at the Auto Teller Machine (ATM)
- Be alert at all times and if you see anything suspicious abandon your transaction and leave.
- If an ATM is poorly lit, find another one, preferably one in a bank and not open to the street.
- Never give your PIN to anyone, not even a bank official or security person.
- Do not count your cash withdrawal at the machine.
- Never accept assistance from a stranger.

It must also be said that you need to be cautious and aware of your surroundings when stopping at many remote or lonely view sites or similar locations. Look for and heed warning notices about quiet or lonely beaches or walks.

chapter eight

BUSINESS BRIEFING

BY WAY OF INTRODUCTION

The South African economy is strong and stable. The South African Rand (ZAR) has strengthened to its best level in years, and consumer inflation is way down, as is the prime interest rate. Business is a vibrant affair, but it is constantly changing, evolving, developing, as is just about everything in the country. It has always been said of South Africa that it had one foot in the First World and the other in the Third, and now the terminology might read the North and the South. Official speeches tend to refer to the country as "developing," meaning the South; but the country undeniably has far too many aspects of the North in it for such comfortable pigeonholing.

There are, as we have seen, two economies—a formal one, in which you are likely to become involved if you are intending to invest or do business in the country, and the informal one. The formal economy is very much like economies around the world, but some of the differences will be dealt with in this chapter. The informal

economy is typified by the street economy, described in Chapter 2. With an unemployment rate hovering around 40 percent, there are certainly many millions of people surviving, and often making a comfortable living, in the informal sector. There are obviously those at the level of the car guards and windshield washers, but there are also those with their own small one-person businesses who provide a product or a service that is needed in a community and that is not available from the formal sector.

BLACK ECONOMIC EMPOWERMENT (BEE)

BEE is probably the most important issue facing the South African economy, for both the domestic businessperson/investor and the would-be foreign one. Without a full understanding of what it is all about, there is little point in even taking the first step. BEE, as defined in the government's declared Strategy for Broad-Based BEE, is "an integrated, coherent socio-economic process which contributes directly to the economic transformation of South Africa, bringing about significant increase in the number of black people who manage, own, and control the country's economy as well as significant decreases in income inequalities." This process is supposed to include human resource development, employment equity, enterprise development, preferential procurement, and investment, ownership, and control of enterprises and economic assets.

Many of these points are covered directly by legislation, including the Skills Development Act, the Employment Equity Act, the Preferential Procurement Act, and the Broad-Based Black Economic Empowerment Act. Much of this legislation has to do with concepts that would be familiar to many overseas visitors, like affirmative action and quota systems. They speak for themselves, except perhaps to say that quotas are covered by the so-called Balanced Scorecard. This means that a business must be able to show that it has a "balanced" workforce of ethnic groups (races) and genders, and also the disabled.

(South Africa has made huge strides in both gender equalization and bringing the disabled, both physically and mentally, on board as full members of society.)

There are bodies like SETA, the Sectional Education and Training Authorities, which are attached to every sector of the economy, providing vital skills training for those who need it. There are many who need it. Of the 508,000 "learners," as school pupils are officially known, who wrote the high school graduation exam in 2005, 68.3 percent passed. Seventeen percent of them received a university "endorsement," and more than 50 percent of the others face no chance of getting a job for a variety of reasons, including a lack of the necessary skills and simply because not enough jobs are being created.

The concept of SMME (Small, Micro, and Medium-sized Enterprises) is important in the economy, often linked to BEE because so many of them are Black-owned. It should be noted that about half the South African work force is with SMMEs.

WOMEN IN BUSINESS

What applies to the rest of the new South African society tends to apply here. Women are on their way up. There are still glass ceilings, but more and more women, particularly Black women, are bursting through them. A recent International Business Owners' Survey gave South Africa the third-highest proportion of companies employing women as senior managers, with 26 percent of total senior management posts being filled by women, giving the country the eighth-highest proportion of women in senior management posts.

PERSONAL CONTACTS

There is without doubt a strong Old Boys' Club that runs through the various racial circles, and there is also a strong tribal factor in the Black business community. There is a lot of nepotism in big business and that would seem to be a fact of life. However, BEE being such an important factor, generally speaking sound personal contacts tend to outweigh nepotism.

BRIBERY AND CORRUPTION

This is another fact of life. There are many laws relating to doing business the right way, and apparently as many ways around those laws, but a good point of departure is to get one of the top consultancies on board, like Deloitte & Touche, KMPG, or PricewaterhouseCoopers, to help you find and stay on the right road. Overseas vacations or fancy cars in return for procurement tenders are becoming more difficult, particularly in a growing (but not always successful) climate of whistle-blowing.

A major issue facing business is fraud, the so-called "white-collar crime." A recent survey showed that South African companies are twice as likely to face fraud activity as their overseas counterparts, with 83 percent of those companies polled having already experienced fraud. A huge step in the right direction as far as this and many other aspects of the economy are concerned was FICA, the Financial Intelligence Centre Act, which threw a blanket of control over many financial dealings previously not quite so vigorously supervised, very much in line with many other international controls introduced since 9/11. This also led to the Amnesty of 2003/4, which gave tens of thousands of South African residents who had illegally squirreled funds abroad, "just in case," the opportunity to come clean and declare all.

Happily there is a national hotline, Tip Offs Anonymous (0 800 003312), covering instances of bribery and corruption, white-collar crime, extortion, and the rest, with information being passed on to the company or the relevant authorities.

DRESS CODE

When in any doubt, a jacket and tie, or for women a smart business outfit, is appropriate, conveying a sense of competence rather than casualness. It has been pointed out that Black South Africans tend to be very dress conscious and may well base their first impression of you on the way you look. They are often fashion leaders with a "trendy" approach.

An invitation to a function may read "Formal [or Black Tie] or Traditional." The first part is obvious—just remember that South Africans, like most other people, love dressing up—but traditional means ethnic, be it African, Asian, or anything else appropriate (but not fancy dress!). Traditional African can be very smart, very funky, or very dramatic, but you're likely to be in for a surprise and a fashion treat. If the invitation says "smart/casual," it is just that, and you should avoid jeans, shorts, and sandals.

For meetings in the bush (discussed shortly), the code is, of course, informal. Remember that the day's business may end with a game drive, therefore natural colors are preferred (yes, khaki, naturally), as wildlife tends to be startled by bright apparel, particularly white.

MEETING AND GREETING

Black Africans can be very casual, but they can also be very formal. One should always use the title of the people one is meeting, especially for business. So, it is always "Mr.," "Mrs.," or "Miss" so and so, and never the first name unless he or she indicates that that is what is preferred.

Name tags at meetings are a blessing, as many South African last names (and even first names) can be very difficult to pronounce. That special African handshake is covered on pages 84-5, but it should be noted that the hand should not be too quickly withdrawn, as a brief lingering will indicate respect and an interest in getting to know the person. When first being introduced, don't be too direct, and start your meeting with some general questions and small talk that has nothing to do with the real business at hand. Be a listener.

A business meeting may take any of the forms to which you are used, but you may also be invited to a *bosberaad*. This is literally a "bush conference," usually in a game or nature reserve, usually fairly informal, although structured, and really more of a brainstorming or "getting-to-know-you" session than a formal conference. These sessions were used to great effect during the run-up to the changeover in South Africa, with people from all conceivable backgrounds being invited to *bosberade* to get to know each other. *Indaba* is another word you may hear. This is also a get-together, but it may be a formal conference or as informal as a quiet drink to discuss business.

BUSINESS ENTERTAINMENT

Generally the days of the power business lunch, starting with martinis and ending with cigars and brandy, are over. Lunch, or even working breakfasts, are more likely to be in a coffee-shop atmosphere with soda rather than chardonnay. Once a deal has been concluded, however, it is a different story, and a dinner in a restaurant is appreciated. That said, big business can and will spend lavishly on product launches and promotions, but always remember that great truth, "There ain't no such thing as a free lunch."

PRESENTATIONS

Although flip charts and overhead projectors are still used, generally speaking presentations in South Africa tend to be highly sophisticated.

Power Point presentations are the norm, with the laptop being almost as ubiquitous as the cell phone, and this may be in an ultramodern conference center or in that *bosberaad* situation. Videoconferencing is a common occurrence here, particularly with overseas parent companies.

NEGOTIATIONS, CONTRACTS, AND DISPUTES

Because legislation pertaining to business in South Africa is complex, the visiting businessperson is strongly recommended to take on a South African partner, and to make sure that he or she is present when it comes to contracts, negotiations, and any follow-through.

Negotiations may be formal or informal and all that we have already said about conducting business applies here. When it comes to contracts, they tend to be taken seriously, so make sure they are right in the first place. Although there is some legal precedent for e-mail contractual arrangements, it is still wise to stick to the signed document format if in any doubt. However careful one may be, disputes can occur. Remember, too, that South Africa has a sophisticated trade union movement and there is a full system of dispute management, arbitration, and the like. Again, it would be useful to have an internationally recognized consultant on board.

SOME SOUTH AFRICAN FIRSTS

If you want to compete with South Africans, this is what you might be up against!

Pratley's Putty—it went to the moon

The world's first automatic popcorn vending machine

Saswitch—ATM access for all bank clients

Computicket—the first computerized ticketing system in the world

Sasol—oil (and all its by-products) from coal

The Scheffel bogey—a revolutionary train carriage wheel assembly

The Disa phone—the first push-button telephone in the world

The waterless toilet

Dolosse—the interlocking breakwater units now used worldwide

Kreepy Krauly, and other such pool-cleaner look-alikes

A Braille wine bottle label—a world first?

The heart transplant (1967)

PUNCTUALITY

Vital in any business, but remember that things can, and do, frequently operate on what is known as African Time, which has nothing to do with Greenwich Mean Time. For details see page 85.

For government regulations on starting up a business, there are Web sites recommended on page 165.

chapter nine

COMMUNICATING

LANGUAGE—HERE'S THAT RAINBOW AGAIN!

Nowhere is the Rainbow Nation more evident than in the line-up of official languages. There are now no fewer than eleven official languages in South Africa—in alphabetical order, Afrikaans, English, isiNdebele, Sepedi, Sesotho, Setswana, SiSwati, Tshivenda, isiXhosa, Xitsonga, and isiZulu. The lingua franca for most spheres of life is English, although Afrikaans is widely spoken in most communities. As far as home language is concerned, isiZulu is by far the most widely spoken (about 25 percent of the population), followed by Xhosa, and Afrikaans (spoken not only by Afrikaners, naturally, but by most of the Colored community as well).

English as a home language is spoken by about 7 percent of the population. That is not the end of it, however. The San or Bushmen peoples speak many different languages and there are other

languages among indigenous peoples such as the
Nama of the Northern Cape. Local communities
with origins elsewhere make a linguistic
contribution too. Indians speak a variety of their
own languages, as do Chinese South Africans, and
then there is the huge Portuguese community, the
Greeks, Italians, Germans, and many others.
There are many different languages from the rest
of Africa too, as immigrants, legal and otherwise,
stream southward to the alleged pot of gold at the
end of the Rainbow.

South Africans are remarkable linguists. Most
are bilingual at least, speaking their home
language plus one other, or more, and many
Blacks will speak their home language and English
and Afrikaans as well. There is now a definite
move toward encouraging the culture of the
African languages, in terms of literature and
education, for example.

South Africans are generally friendly and
polite, and you will notice that a frequent
preamble to any communication will be the,
"Hello, how are you?" ritual already discussed. It
may seem a little silly, but it is a real icebreaker
and often creates a "feel-good" situation. You will
also find in country and small town situations
that people will frequently greet you as they pass,
usually a simple, "Good morning," or "*Dumela*,"
or "*Sawubona*." A similar response is all that is

needed. Because much of South Africa is in dire need of rain much of the time, it is a guaranteed topic of conversation. It is even a Sesotho greeting and toast, "*Khotso! Pula!*" "Peace and rain!"

SOME COMMON WORDS AND TERMS

There are many words and terms in common usage from a dozen or more languages, many of which will be recognizable, many not. Here are a few of the latter.

Ag! – particularly, *Ag, man!* Simply a South Africanism from the original Dutch

Babbalas – a hangover

Bakkie – a utility vehicle, small truck

The Boeing's gone over – meaning, it's time for a drink (rural legend that the first aircraft of the day in many remote areas was the noon flight to Windhoek, definitely time for a drink)

Boer – literally, a farmer, but also a derogatory term for Afrikaners used particularly by Blacks

Bra **or** *bru* – brother, as in America

Dagga – *Cannabis sativa*, marijuana, hemp

Dankie – "thank you" in Afrikaans, or *baie dankie,* "thank you very much"

Eish! – an African exclamation

Hau! – an exclamation of surprise

Howzit? – hello and how are you?

I beg yours? – I beg your pardon?

Indaba – a meeting, conference, talk shop

Ja – pronounced "ya," is simply "yes" in Afrikaans, but almost universal in use

Ja/nee – yes/no, or maybe

Jol – pronounced with a J as in Jim, means play, game, fun—"It's a *jol*!" "It's fun!"

Just now – not right now, but in a little while, although that could mean a considerable period of time

Lekker – anything from great! to nice

Loose – if you are asked for "a loose," it means a single cigarette. "Looses" are often sold by pavement vendors, or at traffic lights

Man – this is used as punctuation in white English, particularly as an exclamation "Man, it's hot!"

The *manne* – the boys, the guys

Mlungus – White people, not necessarily derogatory

Nog 'n piep! – another one! Another "hooray!" Shouted immediately after, "Three cheers!" making it "Four cheers!"

Now now – almost immediately, although it could also mean a considerable period of time

Sefrica **and** *Sefafricans* – it's an accent thing, simply South Africa and South Africans

Shame, **or** *Ag, shame* – a gooey expression of pleasure like, perhaps, "Sweet!" when applied to a baby or a puppy

Sharp or *Sharp sharp* – great! good!

Sies! – an expression of distaste, like *yugh*!

Stoep – veranda, porch

Too much! – especially, *Hau, too much!* May not mean an excessive amount, but rather "plenty." It may also mean "great!".

Viva! – "long live," a revolutionary hangover

Waitron – the ultimate in political correctness, this is neither a waiter nor a waitress, both apparently sexist, but a super, gender-free *waitron*!

SOME VERY "COMMON" WORDS AND TERMS

Because of its linguistic diversity, and probably "attitude," South Africa and its languages are rich in expletives. The traveler will hear many of them, will probably not understand them, and should not repeat them. All the old familiar ones are here, and sometimes used with remarkable ease. Do not be surprised if a shop assistant (for example, a supermarket counterman describing the state of his "fresh" produce) should use a four-letter word that would be totally taboo at home. Cape Town's flower sellers are supposed to be among the greatest exponents of the gentle art of the expletive, as are many motorists. As far as race is concerned, it is obviously highly sensitive—do use the ethnic terms used in this book.

BODY LANGUAGE

Body space, or the individual's comfort zone, may seem somewhat limited here. People do tend to crowd closely together, which comes quite naturally and is part of the local makeup.

The usual ranges of finger, hand, and arm gestures that are normally associated with obscene suggestions are also present and frequently used, particularly by motorists (ignore them). However, there are a number of other signs that the visitor may find puzzling.

One will frequently observe groups of men standing or sitting at a particular spot, usually near a traffic intersection, on a regular basis. As vehicles, particularly *bakkies*, drive past the men will raise one forefinger. This is a reflection of the unemployment situation, and as these are men trying to earn an honest living, the single digit basically means, One Man, One Job, One Day. Frequently, if those waiting are lucky, a vehicle will stop, there will be hurried negotiations on skills needed and remuneration, and the men will jump on the back.

One will more frequently see groups of people or individuals standing beside the road holding up that forefinger. This time they are waiting for a minibus taxi and the single digit means one person wanting to go to town, two digits means two and so on. Taxi hand signals (meaning the hand signals of would-be passengers—taxi drivers do not believe in making hand signals themselves) vary from region to region and city to city, but some are highly imaginative. If one wants to head for the beach, or a seaside town, one imitates the motion of waves with one's hands and forearms, palms down.

Someone "thumbing a lift" by the way, will not necessarily hold up a fist with the extended thumb and jerk it in the desired direction of travel—the fist and thumb will be held out and down, with the thumb pointing in the wanted direction. Regardless, do not under any circumstances pick them up.

Many Black people when handing over or receiving something with either hand, will touch the other hand to the bottom of the arm being held out. This is a sign of respect, but don't try to copy it, just appreciate it.

The visitor will almost certainly notice Black men walking down the street holding hands, or standing chatting and holding hands. This is not what it may seem; it is perhaps simply another expression of *ubuntu.*

If a "bikey" roars passed you in black leather splendor or otherwise and extends an arm out and down and featuring a fingered V sign, it is either a friendly greeting from a fellow King of the Road or he is thanking you for pulling over to let him pass (don't reciprocate with the V sign unless you are another bikey!). Many South African bikers, by the way, despite their fearsome appearance, are members of "gangs" that do some remarkable charity work.

The ultimate in South African body language is the *toyi toyi*. This has almost become a national dance. It started back in the protest days as a gesture of defiance, perhaps, and now although it is still used in that situation (you will see it at protest marches, trade union rallies and picket lines, and similar occasions), you will also see it at sports gatherings, for example. Basically, one knee is lifted high and you hop two or three times on the other foot, then the other knee is raised and you hop on the opposite foot; this is repeated *ad delirium*. If you must try it, make sure it is in the correct social context.

LAUGHING AT THEMSELVES

Yes, they can and do. South African jokes abound, with just about every sector of the broader society coming in for a drubbing sooner or later. Political satire over the years has been untouchable (well, almost) with some remarkably clever, funny, not to mention brave, characters coming to the fore. Perhaps the best known of them all is Pieter-Dirk Uys; all (yes, really all) of South Africa's politicians have at some time or another been the butt of his extraordinary mimicry and wit. Uys (or Evita Bezuidenhout, his favorite *persona*) has been on the South African scene seemingly forever, and he is still there, and enjoyed by all, right now.

THE CELL PHONE CULTURE

Cell phone culture is alive and very well in South Africa, and has been for some years. There are three competing networks, although the competition does not appear to have benefited consumers by way of price cuts. Cell phone rates are high.

The cell phone is arguably the most important fashion accessory at most levels of society, and an essential lifeline among many of the lower income groups. We need not discuss the fashion accessory aspect—the average visitor will be familiar with that—but in a large country like South Africa, with tiny communities and individual homesteads scattered all over the landscape making the provision of landline telephones a costly and difficult affair, the cell phone has been, sometimes literally, a lifesaver.

Wherever there is a signal the phenomenon of the public cell phone stall, usually an ex-shipping container, will appear. This provides a useful service to the community, but cell phones are enormously popular everywhere, despite their cost. There is one particular area where they are a public menace, and that is in the car, as mentioned in the section on Driving, above. Also, the visitor may find their constant and indiscriminate use an irritation—they ring in the cinema or theater, in the restaurant, and at private dinner parties, in fact anywhere, any time, and bans appear to mean nothing.

The Tomato Lady

A couple of years ago I was walking down the main street of Simonstown, the naval base on the Cape Peninsula, with a friend. We spotted a shabbily dressed old woman squatting on the sidewalk selling neat piles of tomatoes. My friend wanted some, and was negotiating a price when a cell phone rang. My friend dived for her handbag, I dived for a jacket pocket, and the old woman dived into the voluminous depths of her tattered dress; it was hers. As we have said, the cell phone brings modern communication to everyone, including the Tomato Lady.

The latest statistics indicate that up to 77 percent of South Africans use cell phones, although usage is not the same in all communities. The number of cell phones in South Africa is way above the world average.

Cell phones may be rented at most major airports and other travelers' facilities, but if you are staying for any length of time, buying a cheap phone may be more cost-effective. All calls are on a pay-as-you-go basis.

LANDLINES, INTERNET, AND MAIL

There is only one telecommunications provider in South Africa and it is Telkom, a public utility with a certain percentage of private shareholders. Government has approved the introduction of a second provider, but exactly how or when this should happen has yet to be decided. Up to 58 percent of South Africans have landlines, compared to 85 percent in 1996, an indication of the phenomenal increase in the use of cell phones.

The growth in the number of computers is also considerable, with an estimated 900,000 South Africans using the Internet every day, and there are Internet cafés in most cities and towns, including some remarkably small places.

The Post Office is a public utility company that runs postal and related services across the country and overseas, reasonably efficiently. Many smaller post offices and agencies have been closed in recent years and there is talk of privatizing the operation completely. The Post Office competes with a number of private organizations, such as PostNet, for example, and the major international and local courier companies.

CONCLUSION

It has been said that once you have lived in Africa you cannot comfortably live anywhere else, that once you have the dust of Africa between your toes, it is there forever. It is the smell of that dust and of chilies, of late rains on dirt streets, of wood smoke in the chill morning air, of grilling meat on a warm evening in the bush, or in a city garden. It is the sound of the cicadas, the deep belly roar of a lion, or a street vendor selling today's newspaper. It is the feeling of sweat running down your back, or a mosquito on your ear. It is the sight of a sunrise over the Indian Ocean or a sunset on the sands of the Kalahari. It is the feel of Africa. You need to be here, in South Africa, to experience it.

South Africa is described as a World in One Country and the Rainbow Nation, but it is not an easy country to understand, or one to which the visitor may easily adjust. It has come through fire, and although there is still considerable heat, it is doing pretty well, thank you, in an unstable world. South Africans may seem an aggressive bunch, but at heart they are friendly and hospitable, and the visitor is likely to experience the latter and not the former. The warmth, vitality, magnanimity, and the spirit of *ubuntu* that informs the new South Africa make it a country full of hope and opportunity.

Further Reading

AA Guides, Self-Catering Getaways, and *Hotels, Lodges, Guests Houses and Bed & Breakfasts,* 2005/2006, published by the Automobile Association.

Bulpin, T.V. *Discovering Southern Africa.* Muizenberg: Discovering Southern Africa Productions, 1992 (and later editions).

Derwent, Sue, and Roger and Pat de la Harpe (photography). *Peoples of the South.* Cape Town: Sunbird Publishing, 2001.

Derwent, Sue, Barry Leitch (consultant), and Roger and Pat de la Harpe (photography). *Zulu.* Cape Town: Struik, 1998.

Lewis-Williams, David. *Bushmen—A Changing Way of Life.* Cape Town: Struik, 1991.

Morris, Donald. *The Washing of the Spears.* London: Jonathan Cape, 1966.

Pakenham, Thomas. *The Boer War.* Johannesburg: Jonathan Ball, 1979.

Schneider, Martin (ed.). *Madiba—A Celebration.* (Nelson Mandela) Sandton: Schneider and Twidale Publishing, 1997.

The Mail&Guardian A-Z of South African Politics, Editors Paul Stober and Barbara Ludman, Jacana Media, 2004.

Useful Web Sites

www.about-south-africa.com (general information)

www.gcis.gov.za (Government Communication and Information System)

www.ghasa.co.za (Guest House Association of South Africa)

www.gov.za (all Government departments, etc.)

www.mg.co.za (*Mail&Guardian* on-line weekly newspaper)

www.news24.com (general news)

www.southafrica.info (general information)

Index

Acknowledgments

With special thanks to my wife and assistant, Sue, for endless help and
support; Dr. Anthony Barale, and Marilyn Dougall Thomas, for their very
special input; and then Dave Bunyard, Dave Estment, Victor Nhlumayo,
and Michael Nkosinathi Diya, for their valuable contributions.